BY THE EDITORS OF CONSUMER GUIDE®

FAVORITE Mexican BRAND NAME RECIPES

BEEKMAN HOUSE
New York

Contents

Copyright © 1983 by Publications International, Ltd.
All rights reserved. This book may not be reproduced or quoted
in whole or in part by mimeograph or any other printed means
or for presentation on radio or television without written
permission from:
  Louis Weber, President
  Publications International, Ltd.
  3841 West Oakton Street
  Skokie, Illinois 60076
Permission is never granted for commercial purposes.

  This edition published by:
  Beekman House
  Distributed by Crown Publishers, Inc.
  One Park Avenue
  New York, New York 10016

Cover Design: Linda Snow Shum

Library of Congress Catalog Card Number: 83-61088
ISBN: 0-517-40834-1

Manufactured in the United States of America
10 9 8 7 6 5 4 3

COVER RECIPES
Front Cover:
Top Left: "Dessert Fruit Taco"
         Lawry's Foods, Inc.
Bottom Left: "Betty Crocker® Taco Salad"
         General Mills, Inc.
Right: "Health Valley® Enchiladas"
         Health Valley Natural Foods
Back Cover:
"Chilly Day Chili"
Heinz U.S.A.

Introduction

A gigantic collection of *your* favorite Mexican recipes, deliciously combined into one cookbook. Hundreds of recipes have been collected from food manufacturers across the country—the recipes you remember from package labels or from newspaper or magazine advertisements.

Right at your fingertips are hundreds of recipes for Mexican favorites. For starters you might choose a cool, creamy guacamole or a plate of cheesy nachos. How about a zesty, chilled Gazpacho soup or a hot and hearty Mexicali Bean Pot? There are tortilla dishes galore; sample the huge selection of tacos, enchiladas, burritos and more! You'll find a chili recipe to suit every taste, and main-dish taco salads to perk up any meal. With such a variety, you'll want to try several—like Mexican Corn Bread, Pineapple Empanadas or maybe a delicious Classic Almond Flan. Mild or spicy, savory or sweet, there's a recipe to suit your every Mexican cooking need.

With all these delicious Mexican recipes at hand, you can put together a festive Mexican meal in no time. Main dishes, salads, soups, appetizers, desserts and more—a complete collection.

An easy-to-use INDEX is provided so that you can locate a recipe by its title, by the brand name product used in the recipe, or by the main food ingredient, such as "chicken."

For your convenience, an address directory of all food manufacturers listed in the book has also been included (see ACKNOWLEDGMENTS). The recipes in this book are reprinted exactly as they appear on the food packages or in the advertisements. Any questions or comments regarding the recipes should be directed to the individual manufacturers for prompt attention. All of the recipes have been copyrighted by the food manufacturers and cannot be reprinted without their permission. By printing these recipes, CONSUMER GUIDE® is *not* endorsing particular brand name foods.

Appetizers

ReaLime® Guacamole

2 medium ripe avocados, seeded and peeled
2 tablespoons **REALIME®** Lime Juice from
    Concentrate
1 tablespoon finely chopped onion
1 teaspoon seasoned salt
¼ teaspoon hot pepper sauce
¼ teaspoon garlic powder

In medium bowl or blender, mash avocados. Add remaining ingredients; stir well. Chill thoroughly to blend flavors. Serve with tortilla chips or fresh vegetables. Garnish as desired.

Makes about 1½ cups

VARIATIONS:

Add one or more of the following ingredients to Guacamole: sour cream, crumbled bacon, coarsely chopped water chestnuts, chopped tomato, chopped mild or hot green chilies.

Easy Guacamole Dip

Peel and pit 1 large ripe avocado. Mash with a fork. Add 1 Tbsp. fresh lemon juice, and 1 to 2 chopped green chiles or **TABASCO® Sauce** to taste. Serve with **JENO'S® PIZZA ROLLS.®**

Makes ¾ cup

Olé Guacamole Dip

1 ripe avocado, mashed
¼ cup dairy sour cream
½ teaspoon fresh grated **SUNKIST® Lemon** peel
1 tablespoon fresh squeezed **SUNKIST® Lemon** juice
½ teaspoon instant minced onion
½ teaspoon garlic salt
¼ teaspoon salt
¼ teaspoon chili powder
Dash hot pepper sauce
1 small tomato, diced

In bowl, combine all ingredients; mix well.

Makes about 2 cups

Guacamole Dip (or Salad)

¼ cup grated onion
½ teaspoon garlic salt
3 large ripe avocados
1 tablespoon lemon juice
1 tablespoon picante sauce
1 teaspoon **GEBHARDT®'S Chili Powder**
Salt to taste

Remove avocado skin and seed. Mash avocados with fork in bowl until smooth. Blend in onion, salt, lemon juice, picante sauce, garlic salt and chili powder. Serve as a dip or on a tomato slice on top of a lettuce leaf as a salad.

Note: If holding for later serving, place in refrigerator and cover with plastic wrap to keep from turning dark.

3

Dieters' Guacamole with Corn Chips

1 pound asparagus (2 cups)
1 tablespoon fresh lemon juice
1½ tablespoons finely chopped onion
1 medium tomato, chopped
1 teaspoon salt
½ teaspoon **SWEETLITE™ Liquid Fructose**
¼ teaspoon ground cumin
¼ teaspoon chili powder
⅛ teaspoon garlic powder
Dash TABASCO® Sauce
½ cup sour cream
1 scant tablespoon (1 envelope) unflavored gelatin
¼ cup water
Fat-Free Corn Chips*

1. Wash the asparagus and break off the tough ends. Cut the spears into 1-inch pieces and cook in a steamer until just fork tender, about 4 minutes.
2. Cool the cooked asparagus to room temperature.
3. Put the cooled asparagus and all other ingredients except the gelatin, water and corn chips into a blender container and blend until smooth.
4. Put the gelatin in a small saucepan and add the water. Allow to soften for 5 minutes.
5. Place the pan on low heat, stirring constantly, until the gelatin is completely dissolved. Do not allow it to come to a boil.
6. Add the dissolved gelatin to the blender container and blend on low speed until thoroughly mixed.
7. Pour the guacamole in a bowl and refrigerate until firm.
8. Serve with Fat-Free Corn Chips, as a dip, sauce or even as a salad dressing.

Makes 2 cups

¼ cup contains approximately:
  ½ vegetable exchange
  ½ fat exchange
  36 calories
  8 mg. cholesterol

*Fat-Free Corn Chips

6 corn tortillas
Salt

1. Cut each tortilla into six pie-shaped pieces.
2. Spread the tortilla sections on a cookie sheet and lightly salt them.
3. Bake in a preheated 400° oven for 10 minutes.
4. Remove from the oven and turn each corn chip over and return them to the oven for 3-5 minutes or until crisp.

Makes 36 corn chips

Each 6 chips contain approximately:
  1 bread exchange
  70 calories
  0 mg. cholesterol

Note: If you prefer smaller Fat-Free Corn Chips, cross-cut the tortillas in strips instead of triangles. You may also wish to sprinkle the tortillas with seasoned salt, cumin or chili powder for flavored Fat-Free Corn Chips.

KNOX®

The Guacamole Ring

2 envelopes **KNOX® Unflavored Gelatine**
1 cup water
2 tablespoons lemon juice
1 teaspoon salt
½ teaspoon garlic powder
½ teaspoon hot pepper sauce
4 medium avocados, mashed
¼ cup finely chopped onion

In medium saucepan, sprinkle unflavored gelatine over water; let stand 1 minute. Stir over low heat until gelatine is completely dissolved, about 5 minutes. Stir in lemon juice, salt, garlic powder and hot pepper sauce.

In large bowl, with wire whip or rotary beater, blend gelatine mixture with avocados. Stir in onion. Pour into 5-cup ring mold or individual molds; chill until firm. Serve as a spread for crackers or party-size breads. *Makes about 5 cups spread*

Ortega Guacamole

2 large ripe avocados
2 tablespoons lime juice
½ teaspoon salt
¼ cup minced fresh onion
1 can (4 oz.) **ORTEGA Diced Green Chiles**
1 small tomato, diced

In bowl, with a fork, coarsely mash all ingredients except chiles and tomato. Fold chiles and tomato into mixture. Serve as dip with tortilla chips, as a salad, or as accompaniment or garnish with Mexican food favorites. *Makes about 2 cups*

Bean Dip

1-16 oz. can GEBHARDT®'S Refried Beans
¼ cup chopped onions
1 clove garlic, minced
1 tablespoon oil
¼ teaspoon salt
1 teaspoon GEBHARDT®'S Chili Powder
1 tablespoon GEBHARDT®'S Picante Sauce*
¼ cup water

Heat oil in a skillet and brown onions and garlic. Add refried beans and stir until hot. Stir in salt, picante sauce, chili powder, and water. Simmer about 5 minutes.

*Picante Sauce

If **GEBHARDT®'S Picante Sauce** is not available, use this recipe.

1-10 oz. can tomatoes & green chilies
1 jalapeño pepper, chopped
½ cup chopped onion
¼ teaspoon garlic salt

Pour can of tomatoes and green chilies in a blender or food processor. Add 1 medium chopped jalapeño, without seeds.** Add ½ cup chopped onion and ¼ teaspoon garlic salt. Turn on to "blend" for about 10 seconds.

Serve as a dip by itself or use as hot sauce in cooking other dishes or as a hot sauce over your favorite Mexican food recipes at the table. Keep your leftover in a jar and refrigerate.

**Note: Add half the jalapeño to start with, adding more later to taste.

Refried Beans

2 cans (16 oz. each) GOYA® Pinto Beans, drained
½ cup shortening
2 Tbsp. flour
2 large onions, chopped
2 large tomatoes, chopped
1 clove garlic, crushed
1 can hot chili peppers, minced
1 tsp. salt
Black pepper to taste

Mash beans by hand or blender. Melt shortening in heavy skillet. Add flour and stir until it begins to brown. Combine mashed beans with remaining ingredients, and add to skillet. Cook, stirring, until shortening is completely absorbed and the beans are fairly dry. Cool slightly and mold into a long roll.

THE ORIGINAL WORCESTERSHIRE

Black Bean Dip

1 can (11 oz.) condensed black bean soup
¼ cup dairy sour cream
¼ cup minced onion
1 clove garlic, minced
4 teaspoons LEA & PERRINS Worcestershire Sauce
2 tablespoons chopped parsley

In a medium bowl mash soup. Stir in remaining ingredients except parsley. Cover and chill for 1 hour. Spoon into a serving bowl. Garnish with parsley. Serve with corn chips or crackers.

Rio Grande Dip

1 can (16 ounces) pork & beans in tomato sauce
1 package (3 ounces) cream cheese, softened
1 tablespoon finely chopped celery
1 tablespoon finely chopped onion
1 tablespoon finely chopped green pepper
2 teaspoons hot sauce
1 teaspoon chili powder
1 small clove garlic, minced

In bowl, mash beans with fork; gradually stir into cream cheese. Add remaining ingredients; chill. Serve as a dip with crackers or chips.   *Makes about 2 cups*

Favorite recipe from **Michigan Bean Commission**

Creamy Chile con Queso Dip

1 cup MERKT'S Cheddar Cheese Spread
1 cup MERKT'S Buttery Swiss Cheese Spread
1 cup sour cream
1 12-oz. can chopped green chilles or banana peppers, drained
1 small can black olives, drained & sliced
1 med. tomato, peeled & chopped

Mix the cheeses with sour cream & half of the chopped peppers. In a small baking dish, spread some of the chopped chilles on bottom. Spread the cheese mixture & cover with remaining peppers. Sprinkle with the sliced olives & chopped tomatoes. Bake in 375° oven for 20-25 min. or until cheeses are melted. Serve hot. Decorate with tortilla chips.

Traditional Chili con Queso

1 medium onion, chopped
1 clove garlic, crushed
1 Tbsp. butter or margarine
1 large tomato, finely chopped
½ cup chopped green chilies
½ tsp. oregano
¾ tsp. salt
1 lb. SARGENTO Shredded Cheddar Cheese

Sauté onion and garlic in butter until soft. Add tomato, green chilies, seasonings and cook over low heat or in the top of double boiler. Stir in cheese until it melts. Serve with tortilla chips.*

*Tortilla Chips: Cut corn tortillas in 6 wedges and fry in deep fat until crisp. Drain.

Chili/Chili con Queso Dip

1 medium onion, chopped
2 tablespoons butter or margarine
10 oz. Cheddar cheese, cubed
6 oz. VELVEETA Cheese, cubed
6-8 tablespoons picante sauce
1-15 oz. can GEBHARDT®'S Chili, No Beans

Sauté onion in butter until soft. Add cheeses and cook over low heat until melted, stirring occasionally. Stir in picante sauce then add GEBHARDT®'S Chili, No Beans. Dip in with your favorite tortilla or corn chip.   *Serves 8 as an appetizer*

5

Mexican Cheese Dip for Little Sausages
(Chili con Queso/Las Salchichas)

4 packages (5 oz. each) **OSCAR MAYER Brand Little Smokies***
¼ cup butter (½ stick)
2 containers (8 oz. each) sharp Cheddar cheese spread
½ cup milk or dry white wine (sauterne)
1 can (4 oz.) sauce for tacos
¼ teaspoon hot pepper sauce
¼ teaspoon lemon juice
¼ teaspoon Worcestershire sauce
½ pimiento pod, diced (optional)

Melt butter in skillet; add cheese spread and stir until melted. Add milk (or wine) and remaining ingredients. Stir until blended and heated through. Add **Little Smokies**. Serve with pics when they are heated through. Keep warm over low heat in electric skillet or chafing dish. More liquid may be added to thin sauce, if necessary. *Makes 64*

Note: Little sausages may be heated on a hibachi for dipping. Keep sauce warm in a heat proof container alongside little sausages.

*4 packages (5½ oz. each) **OSCAR MAYER Brand Little Wieners** may be used.

Chili Cheese Spread

3 cups (1 package) grated **HEALTH VALLEY® Raw Milk Longhorn Cheese**
¼ cup yogurt
2 teaspoons **HEALTH VALLEY® Mustard**
1 teaspoon natural soy sauce (Tamari)
¼ teaspoon garlic powder
½ teaspoon chili powder

Combine all ingredients in a bowl and mix thoroughly. Chill. Serve with **HEALTH VALLEY® Herb** or **Stoned Wheat Crackers**. Total Preparation Time: 15 minutes, plus time to chill.
Yield: About 2 cups spread

Peanut Butter Chili Dip

½ cup **SKIPPY® Super Chunk Peanut Butter**
½ cup chili sauce
1 tablespoon horseradish
1 tablespoon lemon juice

In small bowl stir together peanut butter, chili sauce, horseradish and lemon juice. Cover; refrigerate. Serve with raw vegetables.
Makes about 1 cup

Mexicana Layered Dip

2 15 oz. cans **WOLF® Brand Plain Chili**
½ lb. process cheese spread, cubed
½ cup picante sauce
1 cup dairy sour cream
2 tablespoons green onion slices
1 cup chopped tomato
1 medium avocado, chopped

Combine chili, process cheese spread and picante sauce in saucepan; stir over low heat until cheese spread is melted. Pour into 10x16-inch baking dish and top the center with sour cream. Surround the sour cream with chopped tomato and chopped avocado (dipped in lime or lemon juice). Sprinkle chopped green onions over chili mixture and serve.

Hot Chili-Cheese Dip

1 15-oz. can **ARMOUR STAR® Chili—No Beans**
1 4-oz. can chopped green chiles
1 lb. process American cheese, shredded
1 tablespoon Worcestershire sauce
Corn chips

Combine all ingredients except chips; heat, stirring occasionally, over low heat until cheese melts. Serve as a dip with chips.
4 cups

MICROWAVE METHOD:
Combine all ingredients except chips, in 1½-quart glass casserole. Cook, covered, on HIGH 6 minutes, stirring occasionally. Serve as a dip with chips.

Pimiento Cheese Dip

2 cups (8 oz.) shredded process pimiento cheese
½ cup sour cream
1 package (3 oz.) cream cheese, softened
½ cup **OLD EL PASO® Taco Sauce**
1 can (4 oz.) **OLD EL PASO® Chopped Green Chilies**
4 slices bacon, crisp-cooked, drained and crumbled
⅛ teaspoon cayenne pepper
OLD EL PASO NACHIPS® Tortilla Chips

In small mixing bowl, combine pimiento cheese, sour cream, cream cheese, taco sauce and green chilies. Beat until light and fluffy. Stir in crumbled bacon and pepper. Chill. Serve with vegetable dippers and/or **NACHIPS®**.

King Crab Avocado Dip

1 package (6 to 8 oz.) frozen **ALASKA King Crab meat**
1 large avocado
1 tablespoon lemon juice
1 tablespoon grated onion
1 teaspoon Worcestershire sauce
¼ teaspoon salt
1 package (8 oz.) cream cheese, softened
¼ cup dairy sour cream

Thaw, drain and slice crab. In blender container combine avocado, lemon juice, onion, Worcestershire sauce and salt; blend until smooth. Add cream cheese and sour cream; blend well. Fold in crab. Cover and chill. Serve with crisp vegetables or potato chips.

Makes 2 cups dip

Favorite recipe from **Alaska King Crab Marketing Board**

Port Clyde Foods, Inc.

Port Clyde Tapenade with Raw Vegetables

2 cans (3¾ oz.) **PORT CLYDE** or **HOLMES**
  Sardines packed in oil, drained
18 anchovy fillets with oil
24 pitted black olives
4 cloves garlic
¼ cup olive oil
24 capers
1 tablespoon Dijon mustard
¼ cup cognac
¹⁄₁₆ teaspoon lemon juice
Crisp, fresh raw vegetables such as asparagus spears,
  cauliflower or broccoli flowerets, carrot, celery or
  green pepper strips, green onions, snow peas, or
  zucchini slices

Combine sardines, anchovies, olives, garlic and olive oil in blender; blend until smooth. Add capers, mustard, cognac and lemon juice; blend again (add extra oil if consistency is too thick). To serve, spoon sardine tapenade into bowl placed in center of large platter or tray of attractively arranged vegetables.

BOOTH

Mexicali Dip

1 pound **BOOTH® Peeled and Deveined Shrimp**
1 cup chili sauce
2 tablespoons lemon juice
¼ teaspoon salt
1 tablespoon horseradish
1 tablespoon instant minced onion
2 teaspoons Worcestershire sauce
1 tablespoon chives

Cook shrimp according to package instructions. Chill. Combine remaining ingredients and chill to allow flavors to blend. Use as a dipping sauce for shrimp.

El Rio® Nachos

1 can **EL RIO® Tortillas** (10 oz.)
1 can **EL RIO® Jalapeño Bean Dip** or
  EL RIO® Refrying Beans
1 can **EL RIO® Whole Jalapeños**
Cheddar cheese
Salt to taste

Cut **EL RIO® Tortillas** into quarters. Deep fry in shortening until crisp. Drain and salt to taste. Spread **EL RIO® Jalapeño Bean Dip** or **Refrying Beans** on each Tortilla quarter. Place a slice of cheese on top of the **Jalapeño Bean Dip** and top with a small piece of **EL RIO® Jalapeño Pepper**. Place in a 350 degree oven on a cookie sheet until cheese melts. Serve immediately.

Chex®

Nachos

Mexican CHEX®:
5 tablespoons butter or margarine
1¼ teaspoons chili powder
¼ teaspoon seasoned salt
¼ teaspoon onion powder
6 cups **CORN CHEX® Cereal**

Nacho Topping:
1 can (10½ oz.) jalapeño bean dip
4 tablespoons chopped green chilies, undrained,
  divided
4 teaspoons milk
2½ cups (10 oz.) shredded Cheddar or Monterey Jack
  cheese, divided
Paprika

To prepare Mexican **CHEX®**, preheat oven to 300°. In 13 x 9 x 2-inch baking pan heat butter in oven until melted. Remove. Stir in chili powder, seasoned salt and onion powder. Add **CHEX®**. Mix until all pieces are coated. Heat in oven 20 minutes, stirring once. Spread on absorbent paper to cool.*

To prepare Nacho Topping, combine bean dip, 2 tablespoons chilies, milk and ½ cup cheese.

To prepare Nachos, on heat resistant platter, place 3 cups Mexican **CHEX®** in single layer. Using half the bean dip mixture, drop by small spoonfuls over **CHEX®**. Sprinkle with 1 cup cheese and 1 tablespoon chilies. Broil 3 to 4 minutes or until cheese bubbles. Sprinkle with paprika. Repeat with remaining ingredients.

Makes 10 servings

MICROWAVE METHOD:
In large glass mixing bowl cook butter on High setting 60 seconds or until melted. Stir in seasonings. Add cereal. Stir to coat all pieces. Cook on High 4 to 5 minutes or until crisp. Stir every 2 minutes. Spread on absorbent paper to cool. Prepare as for Nachos. Cook on High 2½ to 3 minutes or until cheese is melted.

*Store tightly covered. May be frozen. Thaw in unopened storage container at room temperature.

Bean Dip Nachos

1 10½-ounce can **FRITOS® Brand Jalapeño Bean Dip**
DORITOS® Brand Tortilla Chips
Jalapeño peppers, sliced
Sharp Cheddar cheese, sliced or coarsely grated

Spread **DORITOS® Brand Tortilla Chips** with **FRITOS® Brand Jalapeño Bean Dip**. Arrange on baking sheet. On each chip place a slice or mound of grated cheese. Top with slice of jalapeño pepper. Bake at 400°F. until cheese melts. Serve hot.

Beef 'n Cheese Nachos

1 can (8 oz.) or ½ can (12 oz. size) **LIBBY'S® Corned Beef**
24 crisp round tortilla chips
1 cup (4 oz.) mild Cheddar cheese
¼ cup chopped mild or hot green chilies

Preheat oven to 425° F. Crumble corned beef with fork; sauté until lightly browned. Arrange tortilla chips on ungreased baking sheet. Cover each with cheese, corned beef and chilies. Bake 6-8 minutes or until cheese is melted. *Yields 24 appetizers*

Note: Serve leftover corned beef as taco filling or store in refrigerator for later use.

Super Quesadilla Ranchero

7 medium sized flour tortillas—8 inch
1 can **NALLEY®'S Chili Ranchero**
1½ cups chopped tomatoes
1 onion, chopped
1½ cups grated Cheddar cheese
¼ cup chopped black olives
½ cup sour cream
3 green onions, thinly sliced
Hot sauce, optional and to taste

Place one tortilla in a large square baking dish. Alternate remaining tortillas with fillings as follows:
Layer one—⅓ can **NALLEY®'S Chili Ranchero**
Layer two—¾ cup chopped tomato and ½ cup chopped onion
Layer three—⅓ can **NALLEY®'S Chili Ranchero**
Layer four—1 cup Cheddar cheese and chopped olives
Layer five—Remaining ⅓ can **NALLEY®'S Chili Ranchero**
Layer six—Sprinkle with remaining tomatoes and onions
Layer seven—Sprinkle top with rest of cheese
  Bake at 325° for 45 minutes. Remove from oven and spread with sour cream and evenly distribute green onions over top. To serve, cut into 6 pie shaped wedges and sprinkle with hot sauce if desired. *Serves 4-6*

Homemade Tortilla Chips

3 cups flour
1 cup yellow cornmeal
4 teaspoons baking powder
1 tablespoon shortening
1 egg, beaten
1 cup water
Oil
MORTON® Popcorn Salt

Up to 1 Week or Day Before Serving: In large bowl, mix flour, cornmeal, and baking powder. Mix in shortening with fork. Stir in egg and water to form a stiff dough. Knead 5 minutes. Divide into 4 parts. Roll each into a 10-inch square, about ⅛-inch thick; cut into 2-inch squares. Divide each square into 2 triangles. Fry in 1-inch hot oil (about 360°F.) about 2 minutes, or until golden on both sides. Drain on paper towels. Sprinkle with popcorn salt. Cool. Store in airtight containers or plastic bags.

Just Before Serving: Place tortilla chips in lined basket or on decorative plate. *Makes about 1½ pounds or 200 chips*

Cheese Crescents
(Quesadillas)

Thoroughly moisten one side of an **AZTECA® Corn** or **Flour Tortilla** with water. On wet side, place 2 Tbsp. shredded Cheddar. Fold in half and fry until crisp in ½ inch hot oil. Press edges firmly together with tongs while frying.

Spicy Crescents

Add peppers, pepperoni or salami with cheese.

Appetizer Crescents

Cut tortillas in half then make as above.

Cheese Sandwiches

Make as above, but do not fry. Fasten edges with a toothpick and place on cookie sheet. Cover with foil. Heat in 300° oven for 10 minutes.

Seviche con Two Fingers®

½ cup lemon juice
½ cup lime juice
½ cup **TWO FINGERS® Tequila**
2 small dried red chili peppers
1 clove garlic, pressed or diced
1 teaspoon salt
Dash dill weed
1 pound sole, halibut or any white flesh fish
1 sweet red onion, sliced
Lettuce

Combine lemon and lime juice with tequila. Seed peppers, and finely grind. Add to first mixture, along with garlic, salt and dill. Cut fish in 1-inch pieces, and pour the mixture over. Top with onion slices. Cover and refrigerate for at least 3 hours, until fish is opaque. Serve as an appetizer or as a salad on lettuce.
  Makes about 2⅔ cups

Note: The citrus juices have much the same effect on the white fish meat that boiling the meat does, so it is essentially "cooked."

Seviche

1 pound sole *or* haddock, fresh or frozen, thawed, cut into bite-size pieces
⅔ cup **REALIME® Lime Juice from Concentrate**
¼ cup sliced green onions
2 tablespoons chopped pimiento
2 tablespoons water
1 clove garlic, finely chopped
1 teaspoon salt
¼ teaspoon black pepper
Dash hot pepper sauce
2 cups shredded lettuce

In medium bowl, combine all ingredients except lettuce. Cover and refrigerate 6 hours or overnight. (**REALIME®** "cooks" fish.) Drain; serve on lettuce. Refrigerate leftovers.

Makes about 2 cups, 6 servings

Mini Mexican Pizzas

1 jar (14 oz.) **RAGÚ´®** **Pizza Quick Sauce**, any flavor
3 English muffins, split and toasted
⅓ cup finely chopped onion
2 tablespoons minced jalapeños (optional)
1 cup (about 4 oz.) shredded Monterey Jack cheese
⅓ cup shredded lettuce
½ cup crushed corn chips
½ cup sliced black olives

Preheat oven to 350°F. Spoon 1½ tablespoons **RAGÚ´®** **Pizza Quick Sauce** on each muffin half. Evenly top with onion, jalapeños and cheese. Place pizzas on baking sheet and bake 15-20 minutes or until cheese melts. Top with lettuce, corn chips and black olives. *Makes 6 pizzas*

Mexican Cucumber Sticks

Peel 1 **CALAVO®-BURNAC Cucumber** cut in half. Put a stick through each piece of cucumber (sucker-wise), dip in lemon juice, sprinkle with salt & roll in a mixture of cayenne pepper, paprika and chili powder.

Empañada Grande

Pastry Dough*
1 cup chopped onions
1 large clove garlic, pressed
1 tablespoon vegetable oil
1 pound lean ground beef
½ cup diced tart apple
1 cup diced cooked potato
¾ cup **THE CHRISTIAN BROTHERS®** Brandy
¼ cup raisins
2 teaspoons grated orange peel
1 teaspoon salt
½ to 1 teaspoon dried red pepper flakes
⅛ teaspoon cinnamon
⅛ teaspoon ground cloves
1 egg, beaten

Prepare Pastry Dough; cover and chill. In large skillet over medium heat sauté onions and garlic in oil 5 minutes. Break up and add beef. Cook and stir until beef loses pink color. Drain fat. Add apple; cook and stir 5 minutes. Add potato, ½ cup of the brandy, the raisins, orange peel and seasonings. Cook and stir 5 to 8 minutes until liquid is absorbed. Stir in remaining ¼ cup brandy; cook 2 minutes. Set aside. Divide Pastry Dough in half. On lightly floured board roll one of the halves into a 10-inch circle. Transfer to baking sheet. Mound beef mixture onto center, leaving a 2-inch pastry border. Roll ¾ of the remaining pastry dough into a 9-inch circle. Place over meat mixture. Fold over and crimp edges to seal completely. Roll out the remaining dough and cut into desired shapes for decorating top of empañada. Apply decorations, using

some of the egg for "glue," then brush top with egg and prick with fork. Bake in 375 degree oven 40 to 45 minutes until browned. Serve warm, cut into wedges.

Makes 8 to 10 appetizer servings

*Pastry Dough

In large bowl combine 2 cups flour, 1 teaspoon baking powder and ½ teaspoon salt. Cut in ⅔ cup vegetable shortening until mixture resembles coarse meal. Add 3 to 4 tablespoons water; toss with fork and form into a ball; wrap and chill.

Taco-Mate

Cheese Sticks Olé

2 sticks pie crust mix
4-oz. (1 cup) shredded **TACO-MATE®**
¼ tsp. dry mustard
2 tsp. paprika

Prepare pie crust mix according to package directions. Stir in remaining ingredients until mixture forms a ball. Roll out on floured surface to 16 x 12 x ¼-inch rectangle. Cut into sticks ½-inch wide and 4-inches long. Place on ungreased baking sheet. Bake in hot oven (425°) for 10 to 12 minutes or until golden brown. Remove from baking sheet; cool. *Makes 96 sticks*

Breads

Taco Rounds

1 pound ground beef
1-1¼ ounce pack Taco Seasoning Mix
1 Recipe Cheesy Corn Meal Biscuits*
1 cup grated cheese

Heat oven to 450 degrees. In a skillet, brown ground beef; drain excess fat. Add Taco Seasoning Mix and water according to package directions; simmer for 15 minutes. Make Cheesy Corn Meal Biscuits according to recipe. Cut out and place on lightly greased baking sheet. With lightly floured fingers, press deep indentation in the center of the biscuit leaving a narrow ridge around outside. Fill with ground beef mixture; sprinkle cheese over filling. Bake 10 to 12 minutes.

Makes about 12-14 Taco Rounds

*Cheesy Corn Meal Biscuits

1½ cups sifted **MARTHA WHITE Self-Rising Flour**
½ cup **MARTHA WHITE Self-Rising Corn Meal**
¼ cup shortening
1 cup grated cheese
¾ cup milk

Heat oven to 450 degrees. Stir together flour and corn meal. Cut in shortening until particles are like fine crumbs. Stir in cheese. Add milk and stir with a fork only until dough leaves the side of the bowl. Turn out onto lightly floured board or pastry cloth; knead just until smooth. Roll dough out about ½-inch thick and cut with floured cutter. Place on lightly greased baking sheet.

Makes about 12-14 biscuits

Note: If using **MARTHA WHITE Plain Flour** and **Corn Meal**, add 3 teaspoons baking powder and ¾ teaspoon salt.

9

Stokely's Finest® Mexican Corn Bread

1⅓ cups yellow cornmeal
1⅓ cups all-purpose flour
3 Tablespoons sugar
½ teaspoon baking soda
1 teaspoon salt
2 eggs
1 cup buttermilk
1 can (8½ ounces) **STOKELY'S FINEST®** Cream
   Style Golden Corn
2 Tablespoons bacon drippings
1 medium-size onion, finely chopped
6 strips bacon, cooked and crumbled
¾ cup grated American cheese, divided
1 to 2 Tablespoons chopped green chilies

Preheat oven to 400°F. Butter 9-inch square pan. Combine cornmeal, flour, sugar, baking soda, and salt in large mixing bowl. Beat eggs and stir in buttermilk, corn, bacon drippings, onion, bacon, ½ cup cheese, and chilies. Add to cornmeal mixture; stir until well combined. Pour batter into prepared pan and sprinkle with remaining ¼ cup cheese. Bake 45 minutes.

8 to 10 servings

South of the Border Corn Bread

7 slices **SIZZLEAN®**, cut into ½ inch pieces
8½ ounce can (about 1 cup) cream-style corn
2 eggs
⅔ cup buttermilk
1 cup cornmeal
⅓ cup drippings and melted shortening
½ teaspoon soda
½ teaspoon salt
⅛ to ¼ teaspoon cayenne pepper
1 cup shredded mild American cheese

Panfry pork breakfast strips in heavy oven-proof 10-inch skillet until browned. Drain. Combine remaining ingredients except cheese. Stir in breakfast strips. Pour half of the mixture into the hot skillet. Cover with cheese. Pour remaining mixture over cheese. Bake in 375°F. oven for 30 to 40 minutes or until done.

Yield: 8 to 10 servings

Note: You may substitute ⅔ cup milk mixed with 2 teaspoons vinegar if you have no buttermilk.

OLD EL PASO®

Mexican Corn Bread

2 packages (8½ oz. each) corn muffin mix
2 cans (4 oz. each) **OLD EL PASO®** Chopped Green
   Chilies, well drained

Preheat oven to 400°F. Prepare corn muffin mix according to package directions. Stir in green chilies. Pour into a 9 x 9-inch square pan. Bake for 15 to 20 minutes.   *Makes 6 to 8 servings*

Bisquick®
SOMETHING GOOD ALWAYS COMES OF IT

Mexican Muffins

1½ cups **BISQUICK®** Baking Mix
½ cup yellow cornmeal
½ cup cream-style corn
1 tablespoon sugar
2 tablespoons milk
¼ teaspoon chili powder
1 egg
1 can (4 ounces) whole green chilies, drained, seeded
   and chopped
1 jar (2 ounces) diced pimientos, drained

Heat oven to 400°. Line 12 medium muffin cups, 2½ x 1¼ inches, with paper baking cups. Mix all ingredients; beat vigorously 30 seconds. Fill muffin cups about ⅔ full. Bake until golden brown and wooden pick inserted in center comes out clean, 20 to 25 minutes.   *12 muffins*

VARIATION:

Mexican Corn Bread

Grease round pan, 9 x 1½ inches. Pour batter into pan. Continue as directed.

HIGH ALTITUDE DIRECTIONS (3500 to 6500 feet): Heat oven to 425°. Stir 2 tablespoons **GOLD MEDAL®** All-Purpose Flour into baking mix. Bake about 20 minutes.

Mexican Hot Pepper Bread

5 to 6 cups all-purpose flour
4 cups **KELLOGG'S CORN FLAKES®** Cereal,
   crushed to fine crumbs, *or* 1 cup **KELLOGG'S®**
   Corn Flake Crumbs
1 tablespoon sugar
1 tablespoon salt
2 packages active dry yeast
1½ cups milk
½ cup vegetable oil
2 eggs
1½ cups grated sharp Cheddar cheese
½ cup finely chopped onions
¼ to ½ cup finely chopped hot chili peppers
2 tablespoons margarine or butter, melted

1. In large bowl of electric mixer, stir together 2 cups of the flour, crushed cereal, sugar, salt and yeast. Set aside.

2. In small saucepan, combine milk and oil. Place over low heat until very warm (120° to 130° F.). Remove from heat. Gradually add to cereal mixture and beat until well combined. Add eggs. Beat on medium speed for 2 minutes. Stir in cheese, onions and peppers. By hand, stir in enough remaining flour to make a stiff dough. On well-floured surface, knead dough about 5 minutes or until smooth and elastic. Place in greased bowl, turning once to

grease surface. Cover lightly. Let rise in warm place until double in volume (about 1 hour).

3. Punch down dough. Divide into 4 pieces. On lightly floured surface, roll each to 7 x 10-inch rectangle. Roll up loaves from longer sides. Place on lightly greased baking sheets. Let rise in warm place until double in volume. Make diagonal slits across top of loaves.

4. Bake in oven at 400° F. about 15 minutes or until golden brown. Place on wire racks. Brush with melted margarine. Cool completely.   *Yield: 4 loaves*

®Kellogg Company

Bridgford Mexican Sweet Bread

1 one pound loaf **BRIDGFORD Frozen Bread Dough**
1 cup sugar
1 cup flour
½ cup melted butter
1 slightly beaten egg
1 teaspoon cinnamon

Let frozen dough thaw. Cut dough into 16 pieces and shape each piece into a ball about 1¼ inches in diameter. Place balls on greased baking sheet, 2 inches apart. Flatten balls slightly with the palm of your hand. Brush rolls liberally with melted butter. Mix together sugar, flour, egg, and cinnamon. Spread 1 tablespoon topping on each roll. Let rise until doubled. Bake in 400° oven for 10 minutes or until lightly browned.   *Yield: 16 rolls*

Mexican Sweet Bread

1 recipe Sweet Yeast Dough*
2 cups sugar
2 cups sifted **MARTHA WHITE Plain Flour**
1 cup (2 sticks) butter or margarine, melted
2 eggs, slightly beaten
1 teaspoon cinnamon
Dash of salt

Let dough rise in bowl. Punch down and let rest 10 minutes. While dough is resting, combine remaining ingredients in a bowl and stir to blend. Pinch off pieces of dough and shape into smooth balls about the size of golf balls. Flatten balls of dough by patting out with the palm of your hand, or with a rolling pin, into four-inch circles. Place circles on greased baking sheets about two inches apart. Place a generous tablespoon of mixture in bowl on top of each round, and spread almost to the edges. Let rise until light, about 30 minutes. Bake at 400 degrees for 10 minutes, or just until lightly browned. Remove from baking sheets and cool a few minutes before serving.   *Makes about 32 buns*

*Sweet Yeast Dough for Sweet Rolls and Coffee Cakes

½ cup lukewarm water
2 cakes or packages yeast
½ cup milk, scalded
½ cup sugar
2 teaspoons salt
½ cup shortening
2 eggs, beaten
About 5 cups sifted **MARTHA WHITE Plain Flour**

Dissolve yeast in lukewarm water. Add sugar, salt and shortening to hot milk. Cool to lukewarm; then beat in eggs. Add two cups of flour and beat thoroughly. Stir in dissolved yeast. Add just enough flour to make a soft dough. Turn out onto lightly floured board or pastry cloth; cover with bowl and let rest 10 minutes. Knead until smooth and satiny. Place in greased bowl and lightly grease top. Cover and let rise in warm place until light, about 1½ hours. When light, punch down and let rest 10 minutes. Shape into rolls, coffee cakes or tea rings. Place on greased pans and lightly brush tops with oil. Cover and let rise until light, about 50 minutes. Bake at 350 degrees; 25 to 30 minutes for coffee cakes; 20 to 25 minutes for pan rolls or 15 to 20 minutes for individual rolls.

Note: If using **MARTHA WHITE Self-Rising Flour**, omit salt.

Sweet Brandy Buns

½ cup **THE CHRISTIAN BROTHERS®** Brandy
½ cup diced candied orange peel
½ cup golden raisins
3½ to 4 cups flour
2 packages active dry yeast
¾ cup milk (approximately)
¼ cup vegetable shortening
¼ cup sugar
1 teaspoon salt
2 eggs
Sugar Topping (recipe follows)

In bowl mix brandy, orange peel and raisins; cover and set aside several hours. In large bowl combine 1½ cups of the flour and the yeast. Drain fruit mixture over measuring cup (there should be about ¼ cup liquid). Add enough milk to make 1 cup. Reserve fruit. In small saucepan combine milk mixture, shortening, sugar and salt. Heat to 120 degrees. Add to flour mixture. Beat with electric mixer at low speed 1 minute. Add eggs and beat at medium speed 3 minutes, scraping sides of bowl as needed. Stir in fruit and another 1½ cups of the flour. Turn onto floured board and knead about 8 minutes, adding the remaining flour as needed to make a satiny, non-sticky dough. Form into a ball and place in a greased bowl, turning to coat top. Cover and let rise in a warm place about 1½ hours until dent remains when poked with finger. Meanwhile, prepare Sugar Topping. Punch dough down and form into 12 equal balls. Place, spaced apart, on greased baking sheets. With heel of hand, flatten each ball to a 3-inch circle. Between lightly floured hands, form 1 tablespoon of the topping mixture into a ball. Pat into a 2½-inch circle and place on 1 of the dough circles. Repeat with the remaining topping mixture. With sharp knife cut through topping to make designs. Cover and let rise in warm place until almost doubled, about 1½ hours. Bake in 375 degree oven about 15 minutes until lightly browned and hollow sounding when tapped. Serve warm or at room temperature.
Makes 12 buns

Sugar Topping

In small bowl combine ⅔ cup flour and ½ cup sugar. Cut in ¼ cup softened butter or margarine until mixture resembles coarse meal. Mix in 1 egg yolk to blend thoroughly.

Sopaipillas with Brandy Anise Sauce

2 cups flour
2 teaspoons baking powder
¼ teaspoon salt
2 tablespoons vegetable shortening
6 to 8 tablespoons water
Vegetable oil for deep frying
Brandy Anise Sauce*

In bowl combine flour, baking powder and salt. With pastry blender cut in shortening until mixture resembles coarse meal. Add enough of the water to make a firm dough. Form into a ball and knead for 3 to 4 minutes on lightly floured board. Divide into 8 equal balls. Roll each ball into a 6-inch circle. Let stand 20 minutes. Meanwhile, heat 3 inches of oil to 390 degrees in large saucepan. Fry sopaipillas one at a time until crisp and browned, turning and pushing beneath surface of oil as they puff. Drain on paper toweling. Serve warm with Brandy Anise Sauce for dipping.

Makes 8 servings

*Brandy Anise Sauce

In 1-quart saucepan combine ¾ cup **THE CHRISTIAN BROTHERS® Brandy**, ⅔ cup packed brown sugar, ¼ cup *each* honey and water and 1½ teaspoons anise seeds. Stir over medium heat to dissolve sugar. Bring to boiling and simmer 5 minutes. Cool. Strain, discarding seeds. Cover and store up to 1 week.

Note: For a simpler version, deep fry flour tortillas as in instructions above.

Soups

 Sunshine®

Sunshine® Gazpacho*

3 large red ripe tomatoes
1 peeled clove garlic
¼ cup olive oil
¼ cup red or white wine
1 peeled cucumber (or unpeeled if garden fresh), coarsely chopped
1 cup chicken or beef broth
¼ teaspoon cayenne pepper
Salt and pepper
1 teaspoon lemon juice
1 green pepper, finely chopped
1 stalk celery, finely chopped
Iced water
6 cubes of ice

Garnish:
1 peeled cucumber, chopped
2 chopped scallions
1 cup coarsely crumbled **SUNSHINE® Crackers**

Peel and quarter tomatoes, remove seeds, saving juice. Put tomatoes and juice, garlic, olive oil, wine, cucumber, broth and cayenne into a blender and blend until well pureed. Add salt and pepper to taste, blend again. Add lemon juice and blend again. Pour into a large bowl. Add green pepper and celery and chill

well. Before serving, check seasonings again and if soup seems too strong add up to 1 cup of iced water and stir well. Put an ice cube in each soup bowl and spoon gazpacho over ice. Pass cucumber, scallions and **SUNSHINE® Cracker** crumbs separately.

Yield: 4 to 6 (1 cup) servings

*A blender is required.

REDPACK
Gazpacho
(Cold Spanish Soup)

3 slices bread
3 tablespoons olive oil
2 cloves garlic, minced
1 can (28 ounces) **REDPACK Whole Tomatoes in Juice**
1 tablespoon chicken soup base concentrate*
¼ cup rosé wine
Pinch of salt
1 large cucumber, peeled and finely grated
Juice of 1 lemon
Parsley or cilantro

In blender whir broken up bread to make fresh breadcrumbs. Heat olive oil in skillet; sauté garlic until golden brown; add bread crumbs and mix well. Remove bread mixture from pan and place in deep bowl; add tomatoes and chicken soup base. Use pastry cutter or fork to blend thoroughly. Stir in wine, salt and cucumber. Refrigerate to chill. Serve cold garnished with lemon juice and parsley or cilantro.

Makes about 5 cups thick soup

*Note: 2 chicken bouillon cubes may be substituted.

Florida Gazpacho

3 medium **Florida Avocados**
1 cup *each* chopped cucumber and green pepper
2 tomatoes, chopped
½ cup finely chopped green onion
2 tablespoons chopped parsley
1 clove garlic, mashed
½ teaspoon hot pepper sauce
½ teaspoon salt
⅛ teaspoon pepper
2 tablespoons lime juice
1 quart tomato juice

Peel and cube avocados. In a large bowl, combine all ingredients. Stir to blend; chill.

Makes about 2 quarts (8 servings)

Favorite recipe from **Florida Avocado Administrative Committee**

Aunt Nellie's®
Mexican Bean Soup

1 can (15½ ounces) **AUNT NELLIE'S® Sloppy Joe Sandwich Sauce**
1 can (16 ounces) refried beans
1½ cups water
1 cup chicken bouillon
Corn chips
Sour cream

In large saucepan, combine sandwich sauce, beans, water and bouillon; mix well. Cover. Heat through. Top each serving with corn chips and sour cream. *6 servings*

Black Bean Vegetable Soup

1½ cups Michigan dry black beans*
3 cups water
4 slices bacon, cut into ¼-inch pieces
¾ cup diced celery
1 leek, diced (about ½ cup)
⅓ cup chopped onion
⅓ cup diced carrot
6 cups beef broth
1 ham hock
½ cup red wine
½ cup tomato purée
½ teaspoon oregano
10 peppercorns
3 cloves garlic
3 whole cloves
1 bay leaf
1 cup water
½ cup rice, uncooked

Place dry black beans in a large saucepan with 3 cups water; bring to a boil; boil 2 minutes; remove from heat; allow to stand 1 hour. Drain; set aside.

In a large soup pot, brown bacon until crisp. Add celery, leek, onion and carrot; sauté 8-10 minutes. Add beans, beef broth, ham hock, wine, tomato puree and oregano to soup kettle. Make a bouquet garni using peppercorns, garlic, cloves and bay leaf; add to kettle. Bring to a boil; reduce heat, cover and simmer 2½ hours.

Add 1 cup water and rice, continue cooking ½ hour longer or until rice is cooked and beans are tender. Remove bouquet garni and discard. Remove ham hock and cut meat from bone, return meat to pot. *Makes 2½ quarts*

*Substitute red kidney beans if blacks aren't available.

Favorite recipe from **Michigan Bean Commission**

Mexicali Bean Pot

1 package (12 ounces) dry chick peas
Water
1 cup chopped ham (about 4 ounces)
1 tablespoon margarine or butter
2½ teaspoons **MORTON® NATURE'S SEASONS® Seasoning Blend**
½ teaspoon ground cumin
1 medium onion, sliced, separated into rings
1 can (6 ounces) tomato paste

Day Before Serving: Place chick peas in 3-quart saucepan or Dutch oven. Pour 6 cups boiling water over peas. Let soak 1 hour. Drain. Add 6 cups fresh water. Cover and simmer about 1½ hours, or until chick peas are tender. Sauté ham in margarine. Stir in remaining ingredients; add to chick peas. Cover and simmer 45 minutes longer. Refrigerate.

About 20 Minutes Before Serving: Reheat, covered, until hot and bubbly. Spoon into soup bowls. *Makes 8 cups*

Southern Bean Dip Soup

3 10½-ounce cans **FRITOS® Brand Jalapeño Bean Dip**
1 can beef broth
1 broth can water
3 medium potatoes, peeled and cut in 1-inch cubes
1 cup chopped onion
1 cup chopped celery
1 can whole kernel corn
½ cup chopped green pepper

Mix in a kettle the **FRITOS® Brand Jalapeño Bean Dip**, broth and water. Simmer uncovered for 30 minutes. Add potatoes, onion, celery, corn and pepper. Simmer for 1 hour. Serve hot. *Makes 8 to 10 servings*

Hunt's.

Sopa de Lentejas

1 cup lentils
1 qt. water
5 slices bacon, cut into squares
1 medium onion, chopped
½ cup *each*: sliced carrots and celery
1 (15-oz.) can **HUNT'S® Tomato Sauce**
1 teaspoon salt
1 bay leaf
3 peppercorns
1 beef bouillon cube

Soak lentils in water 30 minutes. In a Dutch oven or heavy kettle, sauté bacon and onions until bacon is crisp and onions are transparent. Add *undrained* lentils, carrots, celery, **HUNT'S® Tomato Sauce**, salt, bay leaf, peppercorns and bouillon cube. Simmer about 1 hour. *Makes 8 servings*

Easy Chili Chowder

½ pound ground beef
¼ cup chopped green pepper
¼ cup chopped onion
1 can (17 ounces) **ROSARITA® Refried Beans**
1 can (10 ounces) **ROSARITA® Enchilada Sauce**
½ cup water
¼ teaspoon salt

In medium saucepan, lightly brown beef with green pepper and onion. Stir in remaining ingredients. Simmer, uncovered, for 15 minutes, stirring several times. *4 servings*

PET.

Tomato Chili Cheese Soup

2 tablespoons vegetable oil
1 onion, finely chopped
4 green onions, finely chopped
1 clove garlic, minced
1 can (10 oz.) **OLD EL PASO® Tomatoes and Green Chilies**
1 can (4 oz.) **OLD EL PASO® Chopped Green Chilies**
1 tablespoon cilantro
2 cups water, divided usage
½ teaspoon salt
¼ teaspoon pepper
1 tall can (13 fl. oz.) **PET® Evaporated Milk**
2 cups (8 oz.) shredded Monterey Jack cheese
1 cup (4 oz.) shredded American cheese
½ cup butter

Heat oil in a large saucepan. Add onion, green onions and garlic. Cook until translucent. Add tomatoes and green chilies, green chilies, cilantro, 1 cup water, salt and pepper. Simmer about 15 minutes. In another large saucepan, combine remaining 1 cup water, evaporated milk, cheeses and butter. Stir over medium heat until cheeses and butter are melted. Add tomato mixture. Stir and simmer over medium heat about 10 minutes. *Caution:* Do not let this mixture boil, it may curdle.

Makes 8 servings

Hearty Chili Soup with Condiments

1 can **NALLEY®'S Chili Picante**
1 28 oz. can whole tomatoes, roughly chopped
1 15 oz. can red kidney beans, drained
4 cups water
1-3 tsp. chili powder—to taste
¼ tsp. cayenne pepper
1 tsp. salt
1 Tbsp. brown sugar
1 Tbsp. Worcestershire sauce
1 tsp. hot red pepper flakes

Condiments:

2 cups grated Cheddar cheese
¾ cup thinly sliced green onions
½ pint sour cream

Combine **Chili Picante**, whole tomatoes and red kidney beans in a 6-qt. sauce pan. Stir in water and heat over high heat until boiling. Reduce heat to simmer and add chili powder, cayenne pepper, salt, brown sugar, Worcestershire sauce and hot pepper flakes. Simmer for one hour. Ladle into heated bowls and serve. Pass condiments around separately for garnishing.

Serves 6-8

Tortilla Soup

2 or 3 **OLD EL PASO® Corn Tortillas**
Oil for frying
2 teaspoons vegetable oil
⅓ cup chopped onion
1 can (4 oz.) **OLD EL PASO® Chopped Green Chilies**
4 cups chicken broth
1 cup shredded, cooked chicken
Salt
1 can (10 oz.) **OLD EL PASO® Tomatoes and Green Chilies**
1 tablespoon lime juice
4 large lime slices

Cut tortillas in 2 x ½-inch strips. Fry tortillas in small amount of hot oil until brown and crisp. Drain on paper towels. Heat 2 teaspoons of vegetable oil in a large saucepan. Add onion and sauté until translucent. Add green chilies, broth, chicken, salt to taste, and tomatoes and green chilies. Cover and simmer 20 minutes. Stir in lime juice. To serve, pour into soup bowls and add tortilla strips. Float a lime slice in the center of each bowl.

Makes 4 servings

Savory Tortilla Soup

Dry at least ½ hour in open air:
    4 **AZTECA® Corn** or **Flour Tortillas** cut in ½-inch x 1-inch pieces
Melt in 2 qt. saucepan:
    2 Tbsp. butter or margarine
Sauté:
    1 large onion, thinly sliced
    3 large cloves garlic, crushed
Add:
    2 13¼ oz. cans beef broth
    1 tsp. salt
    ¼ tsp. dried tarragon

Simmer 15 minutes. Fry tortilla strips until golden. Remove with slotted spoon to paper towels. Divide between four soup bowls. Top each with:
    1 tsp. Parmesan cheese
Stir into soup:
    1 tsp. lime or lemon juice

Pour over tortillas.

Makes 4 bowls

Lindsay.

Mexicorn Chowder

2 tablespoons butter
2 tablespoons flour
1 (10½ oz.) can condensed chicken broth
1 cup milk
1 tablespoon minced onion
1 can mexicorn
1 (2¼ oz.) can **LINDSAY® Sliced Ripe Olives**
⅛ teaspoon fine herbs

Melt butter and blend in flour. Stir in chicken broth gradually. Add milk and onion and cook, stirring until mixture boils thoroughly. Add corn, drained ripe olives and herbs. Serve hot.

Makes about 3 cups

DANNON YOGURT

Green Chile Soup

2 tablespoons butter or margarine
1 tablespoon oil
4 to 5 cloves garlic, finely chopped
1 medium onion, chopped
2 teaspoons paprika
4 cups chicken broth
1½ pounds tomatoes, chopped
1 4-ounce can diced green chiles
¼ teaspoon chili powder
Salt and pepper to taste
2 8-ounce or 1 16-ounce container **Plain DANNON® Yogurt**
4 ounces Jack or Cheddar cheese, shredded
1 tablespoon chopped cilantro or parsley

Melt butter in large stock pot; add oil. Sauté garlic until lightly browned. Remove garlic and set aside. Add onion to butter; sauté until soft. Add paprika; sauté 1 minute. Add chicken broth, tomatoes, chiles, chili powder, salt and pepper. Bring to a boil; reduce heat and simmer 20 minutes. Stir in yogurt slowly; heat thoroughly over low heat. Add reserved garlic. Ladle into soup bowls; sprinkle with cheese and cilantro.   *Serves 6*

Salads

Mexican Salad-Sandwich

1 head **California ICEBERG Lettuce**
12 corn tortillas, fresh, canned or frozen
½ cup corn oil
2 cans (1 pound *each*) kidney beans, drained
¾ teaspoon garlic salt
Dash hot pepper sauce
1 pound ground beef
2 tablespoons butter or corn oil
1 large onion, chopped
1 medium green pepper, chopped
2 cans (8 ounces *each*) tomato sauce
¼ teaspoon crushed oregano
¼ teaspoon pepper
½ cup grated Cheddar cheese

Core, rinse and thoroughly drain lettuce; refrigerate in plastic bag or plastic crisper. Fry each tortilla in hot oil about 30 seconds or until crisp; drain on paper towels. Drain off all but 2 tablespoons oil; add beans, ½ teaspoon garlic salt and hot pepper sauce. Cook and mash beans until thick paste is formed. Brown meat in butter, separating with fork. Stir in onion and green pepper; cook until tender. Add tomato sauce, oregano, pepper and remaining ¼ teaspoon garlic salt. Simmer over low heat 5 minutes. Shred lettuce by halving head lengthwise, then place cut-sides down and cut crosswise. Layer each tortilla with beans, shredded lettuce and meat. Serve with cheese.   *Makes 6 servings*

Favorite recipe from **California Iceberg Lettuce Commission**

Red Kidney Bean Salad

1 cup cubed cheese—American, Cheddar, etc.
⅓ cup chopped green pepper
⅓ cup chopped celery
2 tablespoons chopped onion
2 hard cooked eggs, chopped
1 can (15 oz.) red kidney beans, drained
½ cup **MILNOT®**
1½ tablespoons lemon juice or vinegar
½ teaspoon salt
Dash of pepper
4 tablespoons chili sauce
Salad greens

Place cheese, green pepper, celery, onion, eggs, and beans in bowl. Combine **MILNOT®**, lemon juice, salt, pepper, and chili sauce. Blend until smooth. Pour over vegetables and toss until well coated. Line bowl with salad greens, heap salad on top. Garnish with onion and green pepper rings.

Yield: approximately 6 servings

Zippy Mexican Salad

2 cups (8 ounces) **SKINNER® Elbow Macaroni,** uncooked
¾ cup mayonnaise or salad dressing
½ cup chili sauce
2 tablespoons vinegar
2 teaspoons onion salt
1 teaspoon chili powder
4 to 5 drops hot pepper sauce
2 cups (16-ounce can) red kidney beans, drained
½ cup sliced ripe olives
½ cup minced green onion

Cook Elbow Macaroni according to package directions; drain well. Cool. (Rinse with cold water to cool quickly; drain well.)

Combine mayonnaise or salad dressing, chili sauce, vinegar, salt, chili powder and hot pepper sauce in large bowl; blend well. Add cooled Elbow Macaroni, kidney beans, olives and onion to the mayonnaise mixture: toss lightly until all ingredients are blended. Chill.   *6 to 8 servings*

Nopalitos Salad

1 26 oz. can **LA PREFERIDA® Nopalitos Natural** (cactus), drained, rinsed in cold water
5 oz. red onion, sliced very thin
4 oz. **LA PREFERIDA® Queso Anejo Cheese**, grated (optional)
1 tomato, sliced
1 tsp. cilantro, chopped (fresh)*(optional)
½ garlic clove, minced (optional)
½ cup salad oil
⅓ cup wine vinegar
Salt to taste

Combine all ingredients thoroughly. Chill salad before serving.

*Fresh cilantro is a Mexican-type parsley with a unique flavor and aroma. It is also known as coriander, and if not available, may be substituted with Italian parsley or left out entirely.

Regina.

Gazpacho Salad

Dressing:
½ cup **REGINA Red Wine Vinegar**
1 cup olive oil
1 can (7 oz.) **ORTEGA Green Chile Salsa**
1 teaspoon oregano
1 teaspoon basil
2 bay leaves
½ teaspoon rosemary
½ teaspoon salt

Salad:
3 medium tomatoes, sliced
1 medium red onion, thinly sliced
1 can (7 oz.) **ORTEGA Whole Green Chiles**, sliced crosswise
1 cucumber, thinly sliced
Bibb lettuce
Croutons
Cooked, crumbled bacon
Freshly grated Jack cheese

Thoroughly combine all dressing ingredients. In large bowl, layer tomatoes, onion, chiles and cucumber. Drizzle with dressing. Cover. Refrigerate 3-4 hours. Drain. Serve on lettuce. Garnish with croutons, bacon and cheese. *Serves 8*

Game Point Guacamole Bowl

1 ripe avocado
Lemon juice
¼ cup **DARI-LITE 1% Milk**
1 tablespoon lemon juice
½ cup **DARI-LITE Sour Half-N-Half**
⅓ cup oil
½ teaspoon sugar
½ teaspoon chili powder
¼ teaspoon Mexican Salsa
Dash garlic powder
6 cups torn lettuce
1 12½-oz. can tuna, chilled, drained and flaked
1 cup cherry tomatoes, halved
1 cup tortilla chips
½ cup bias-sliced celery
½ cup **DARIGOLD Cheddar Cheese**, shredded
⅓ cup chopped green onion

Cut avocado in half; remove seed and peel. Mash enough avocado pulp to make ½ cup. Chop any remaining avocado and dip in a little lemon juice to prevent darkening.

For salad dressing combine mashed avocado, milk, 1 tablespoon lemon juice, **Sour Half-N-Half**, salad oil, sugar, chili powder, Mexican Salsa and garlic powder. Beat till mixture is smooth. Stir in chopped avocado. In large bowl toss together torn lettuce, tuna, cherry tomatoes, tortilla chips, celery, Cheddar cheese and green onion. Serve with salad dressing.

Makes 4 main dish servings

Calories: Salad without dressing approximately 205 calories per serving. Dressing is approximately 50 calories per tablespoon.

Gazpacho Garden Salad

½ cup vegetable oil
⅓ cup **REALEMON® Lemon Juice From Concentrate**
2 cloves garlic, finely chopped
1½ teaspoons salt
¼ teaspoon pepper
1 medium green pepper, seeded and diced
2 medium, firm tomatoes, diced
1 medium cucumber, peeled, seeded and diced
½ cup sliced green onion

In 1-pint jar with tight-fitting lid, combine oil, **REALEMON®**, garlic, salt and pepper; shake well. In narrow 1-quart glass container, layer ½ each of the green pepper, tomato, cucumber and onion; repeat layering with remaining vegetables. Pour dressing over salad. Chill 4 hours to blend flavors.

Makes 8 servings

Acapulco Salad

Drain:
    1 can (2¼ oz.) sliced ripe olives
    1 can (8½ oz.) garbanzo beans
    1 can (8¾ oz.) **DEL MONTE Whole Kernel Family Style Corn** (Reserve liquid for other recipe uses)
Using sharp knife, shred:
    ½ head iceberg lettuce
Thinly slice:
    1 bunch radishes
Toss ingredients with:
    Bottled green goddess dressing

Season with garlic salt and pepper to taste. Garnish with shredded Cheddar cheese.

San Giorgio®

Taco Mac Salad

3 cups (8 ounces) **SAN GIORGIO® Rotini**, uncooked
1 pound ground beef
½ cup chopped green pepper
1 package (1¼ ounces) taco seasoning
½ head lettuce, shredded
1 package (5½ ounces) taco flavored corn chips, broken
½ cup shredded Cheddar cheese
Cherry tomato halves or tomato wedges

Cook Rotini according to package directions; drain and keep warm. Meanwhile, brown meat in skillet; add green pepper and sauté until tender. Stir in taco seasoning; mix well. Place shredded lettuce on large platter; layer hot Rotini, corn chips and meat mixture over lettuce. Sprinkle with shredded cheese; garnish with cherry halves or tomato wedges. Serve hot. *About 4 servings*

Betty Crocker® Taco Salad

1 pound ground beef
1 package **BETTY CROCKER® HAMBURGER HELPER®** Mix for Cheeseburger Macaroni
3⅓ cups hot water
2 to 3 teaspoons chili powder
1 large clove garlic, crushed
Dash of cayenne pepper, if desired
6 cups shredded lettuce
1 medium green pepper, chopped (about 1 cup)
2 medium tomatoes, chopped (about 1½ cups)
⅓ cup sliced green onions (with tops)
¼ cup sliced ripe olives

Cook and stir ground beef in 10-inch skillet until brown; drain. Stir in Macaroni, Sauce Mix, water, chili powder, garlic and cayenne pepper. Heat to boiling, stirring constantly; reduce heat. Cover and simmer, stirring occasionally, 15 minutes. Uncover and cook 5 minutes longer.

Place lettuce, green pepper, tomatoes, onions and olives in large bowl; toss with ground beef mixture. Serve immediately or, if desired, cover and refrigerate until chilled, at least 4 hours. Serve with tortilla chips and dairy sour cream if desired.

6 to 8 servings

HIGH ALTITUDE DIRECTIONS (3500 to 6500 feet): Increase hot water to 3½ cups and simmer time to 20 minutes.

Mexican-Style Taco Salad

4 cups coarsely chopped iceberg lettuce
1 pint cherry tomatoes, halved
½ cup pimiento-stuffed green olives, sliced
1 large green pepper, cored and diced (about 1 cup)
1½ cups coarsely shredded Cheddar cheese
1 pound ground beef round
¾ cup chopped onion
1 can (20 ounces) red kidney beans, drained
2 tablespoons red wine vinegar
2 teaspoons ground cumin seed
2 teaspoons chili powder
½ teaspoon salt
¼ teaspoon pepper
1½ cups **PEPPERIDGE FARM® Cheddar-Romano** or **Sour Cream and Chive Croutons**
1½ cups plain yogurt or sour cream

Arrange lettuce, tomatoes, olives, pepper and cheese on a large platter. Chill up to 12 hours. Heat a large skillet over moderately high heat. Add beef and onion and cook, stirring frequently, until

beef is browned and onion is soft. Add beans, vinegar, cumin, chili, salt and pepper. Cook 3 to 4 minutes longer, stirring constantly, until most moisture has evaporated. Cover loosely and let stand 30 minutes. *Just before serving*, spoon meat mixture on top of lettuce mixture; sprinkle with croutons and serve with yogurt or sour cream. *Makes 6 main-dish servings*

Chilli Man® Taco Salad

1 can (15 oz.) **CHILLI MAN®** Chilli
1 small head iceberg lettuce, torn in pieces
1 cup shredded Cheddar cheese
½ cup green onions, sliced
1 tomato, cut in wedges
1 small avocado, cubed (optional)
½ cup sliced green or black olives (optional)
1 cup crushed tortilla chips
½ cup bottled salad dressing or sour cream
½ to ¾ cup taco sauce—as desired

Heat **CHILLI MAN® Chilli;** spoon off excess fat. Toss all ingredients except taco sauce—it may be poured on as desired. Garnish with additional taco chips. *Makes about 6 servings*

Hamburger Helper®

Spicy Hot Taco Salad

1 pound ground beef
1 package **BETTY CROCKER® HAMBURGER HELPER®** Mix for Chili Tomato
3⅓ cups hot water
3 teaspoons chili powder
½ teaspoon dried oregano leaves
½ teaspoon ground cumin, if desired
¼ teaspoon red pepper sauce
Dash of cayenne pepper, if desired
1 large clove garlic, crushed
6 cups shredded lettuce
2 medium tomatoes, chopped (about 1½ cups)
1 medium green pepper, chopped (about 1 cup)
⅓ cup sliced green onions (with tops)
¼ cup sliced ripe olives
1 can (4 ounces) chopped green chilies, drained
Tortilla chips

Cook and stir ground beef in 10-inch skillet until brown; drain. Stir in Macaroni, Sauce Mix, water, chili powder, oregano, cumin, pepper sauce, cayenne pepper and garlic. Heat to boiling, stirring constantly. Reduce heat; cover and simmer, stirring occasionally, 15 minutes. Uncover and cook 5 minutes longer; cool 5 minutes. Place remaining ingredients except tortilla chips in large bowl; toss with ground beef mixture. Serve immediately, or if desired, cover and refrigerate until chilled, at least 4 hours. Serve with tortilla chips and, if desired, dairy sour cream. *6 to 8 servings*

HIGH ALTITUDE DIRECTIONS (3500 to 6500 feet): Increase hot water to 3½ cups and simmer time to 20 minutes.

PREMIUM
Saltine Crackers

Hot Mexican Salad

2 (15-ounce) cans chili with beans
4 ounces Cheddar cheese, grated (about 1 cup)
¼ cup diced green chilies
½ teaspoon liquid hot pepper seasoning
1 large head iceburg lettuce
1 large tomato, chopped (about 1 cup)
½ cup sliced scallions
Dairy sour cream
PREMIUM Saltine Crackers

1. In medium saucepan, combine chili, half of cheese, green chilies and hot pepper seasoning. Cover and simmer 10 minutes.

2. Meanwhile, slice lettuce crosswise into four 1-inch "rafts." Store remaining lettuce for another use.

3. To serve, place lettuce rafts on four individual serving plates. Spoon over chili mixture. Top with remaining cheese, tomato, scallions and sour cream. Serve salad with **PREMIUM Saltine Crackers**.

Makes 4 main-dish servings

Mexican Chef Salad

½ to ¾ pound chopped or coarsely ground cooked **PROTEN® Beef**
½ cup chopped onion
1 tablespoon butter or margarine
15½ ounce can kidney beans, drained
¼ teaspoon salt
1 medium head lettuce, torn into bite-size pieces
4 medium tomatoes, chopped
1 cup (4 ounces) shredded cheese
1 cup French dressing
6 ounces corn chips, crushed
1 medium avocado, peeled and sliced

Cook onion in butter until tender. Add beef and stir to brown lightly. Add kidney beans and salt. Cover and cook over low heat about 10 minutes. Combine remaining ingredients in a large bowl. Add hot beef mixture to salad. Toss lightly and serve immediately. *Yield: 6 to 8 servings (3 quarts)*

Sonoran Luncheon Salad

1 can (6½ oz.) **BUMBLE BEE® Chunk Light Tuna in Water**
½ small avocado, peeled and chopped
⅔ cup shredded sharp Cheddar cheese
¼ cup chopped celery
3 cups shredded lettuce
Crisp lettuce leaves
Salsa*
Broiled Tortilla Chips**

Drain tuna. Combine tuna, avocado, cheese and celery. Mound mixture on shredded lettuce in two salad bowls lined with crisp lettuce leaves. Serve with Salsa on top and Broiled Tortilla Chips.

Makes 2 servings

Calories: 499 calories per serving

*Salsa

1 can (16 oz.) whole tomatoes
¼ cup chopped green chiles
¼ cup chopped onion
¼ teaspoon oregano, crumbled
¼ teaspoon salt
⅛ teaspoon ground cumin

Drain tomatoes reserving ⅓ cup juice. Chop tomatoes. Combine juice and tomatoes with remaining ingredients. Spoon over salads.

**Broiled Tortilla Chips

Cut 2 medium corn tortillas into 12 wedges. Place on cookie sheet and broil until crisp and brown, turning once. *Makes 24 chips*

Mexicali Ham Salad

1 envelope (1¼-oz.) **FRENCH'S® Taco Seasoning Mix**
1 cup tomato juice
¼ cup vinegar
¼ cup oil
2 cups diced cooked ham
1 can (15-oz.) kidney beans, drained and rinsed
2 cups chopped celery
1 cup diced Swiss cheese
½ cup chopped green pepper
Lettuce

Combine seasoning mix, tomato juice, vinegar and oil in covered container; shake to blend. Combine ham, beans, celery, cheese and pepper; add enough dressing to moisten and toss lightly. Serve on lettuce. Refrigerate remaining dressing for use on any green salad, coleslaw or bean salad. *4 to 6 servings*

Arroz con Pollo Salad

1 cup chopped onion
1 tablespoon vegetable oil
2⅔ cups water
1 cup **UNCLE BEN'S® Select Brown Rice**
2 teaspoons chili powder
2 teaspoons salt
½ cup vegetable oil
2 tablespoons vinegar
2 cups diced cooked chicken
1 package (10 ounces) frozen peas, cooked and drained
½ cup ripe olive slices
2 soft California avocados
1 medium tomato, chopped, chilled

Cook onion in oil in large saucepan until tender but not brown. Add water and bring to a boil. Stir in rice, chili powder and 1 teaspoon salt. Cover tightly and cook over low heat until all liquid is absorbed, about 50 minutes. Combine oil, vinegar and remaining salt, mixing well; stir into hot cooked rice with chicken, peas and olives. Chill. To serve, peel, seed and coarsely chop 1½ avocados, reserving remaining half for garnish. Stir chopped avocado and tomato into rice mixture. Top with reserved avocado slices. *Makes 6 main dish servings*

Brandy Fiesta Salad

6 slices (1-inch thick) fresh pineapple, halved, peeled
   and cored
3 oranges, peeled and sliced
⅔ cup **THE CHRISTIAN BROTHERS®** Brandy
⅓ cup sugar
¼ cup water
¼ teaspoon salt
¼ cup white wine vinegar
2 cups shredded green cabbage
2 cups shredded red cabbage
Cilantro or watercress sprigs

Combine pineapple and orange slices in bowl; set aside. In 1-quart saucepan combine brandy, sugar, water and salt. Bring to boiling, stirring. Simmer 5 minutes. Remove from heat. Stir in vinegar. Pour over fruits. Cover and chill several hours, tossing occasionally. Mound cabbage in serving bowl. Arrange fruits over cabbage. Drizzle with brandy mixture. Garnish with cilantro.

Makes 6 servings

Tortilla Dishes

Tortilla Pie

In skillet brown:
    1 lb. ground beef
Add:
    2 cans (8 oz. each) **DEL MONTE Tomato Sauce**
    1 pkg. (approx 1½ oz.) chili seasoning mix
    1 can (2¼ oz.) sliced ripe olives

Simmer.

In round 2-quart casserole, layer alternately:
    6 corn tortillas
    Meat sauce
    1½ cups shredded Cheddar cheese

Top with additional ½ cup cheese. Pour ½ cup water down edge, into bottom of casserole. Cover and bake at 425° F, 20 minutes. Remove cover. Let stand 5 minutes before cutting into wedges. Garnish with sour cream and chiles.

Quesadillas
(Kay-sah-dee-yahs)

1 lb. **JIMMY DEAN® Seasoned Taco Filling**
8, 8-inch flour tortillas
4 cups grated Cheddar cheese
Butter
Guacamole*
Sour Cream
Garnishes: black olives, jalapeños, cherry tomatoes,
   cut in round slices

Sauté **JIMMY DEAN® Seasoned Taco Filling** until brown and crumbly. Drain on paper towel. Sprinkle 4, 8-inch flour tortillas with ½ cup grated Cheddar cheese and spoon over ¼ of filling on each. Top with ½ cup of cheese. Cover with a second tortilla. Melt 2 Tbsp. butter in a large frying pan over medium heat. Lay in filled tortillas and cook until golden brown underneath. Turn and brown other side, as you would a grilled cheese sandwich. Cut into 8, pie-shaped wedges. Garnish each wedge with 1 tsp. guacamole and sour cream. Top each with alternate slices jalapeño, cherry tomatoes and black olives. Serve at once or place in a baking pan uncovered and keep warm in a 250° oven until all are fried.

Serves four as a main course

*Guacamole
(Wah-cah-moh-lay)

2 medium avocados
1 small tomato, chopped
2 Tbsp. minced onion
1 tsp. lime juice
½ tsp. salt
½ tsp. garlic powder

Peel avocados. Mash with a fork. Stir in rest of ingredients.

Port Clyde Foods, Inc.

Holmes Tortilla Rolls

8 tortillas
4 cans (3¾ oz.) **HOLMES** or **PORT CLYDE**
   Sardines or **Fish Steaks** in oil, drained
6 ounces shredded Monterey Jack cheese
1½ cups shredded lettuce
1 cup taco sauce
1 cup sour cream

Pre-heat oven to 350°. Wrap tortillas tightly in foil packet and heat in oven about 10 minutes, or until warm. Place sardines, cheese and lettuce on tortillas, dividing evenly. Spoon taco sauce and sour cream over fillings; roll up tortillas and serve immediately.

Makes 8 servings

La Preferida® Mexican Pizza

2 oz. **LA PREFERIDA® Chorizo***
1 flour tortilla 10 in.
½ cup **LA PREFERIDA® Refried Beans**
2 Tbsp. **LA PREFERIDA® Enchilada Sauce**
10 slices **LA PREFERIDA® Jalapeños**
1 oz. Oaxaca cheese, grated**

Sauté Chorizo until cooked through. Spread tortilla first with Refried Beans, then Enchilada Sauce. Top with remaining ingredients. Place on lightly oiled baking sheet. Bake at 400 F. for 12 minutes.

Makes one 10 in.

*Italian sausage may be substituted.
**Muenster cheese may be used as a substitute.

Wheat Germ Flautas

Cooking oil
4 flour tortillas
1 cup grated Monterey Jack cheese
¾ cup **KRETSCHMER Regular Wheat Germ**
½ cup dairy sour cream
½ cup chopped green onion
½ cup pitted ripe olives, cut into thin wedges
¼ cup chopped green chilies
1 medium clove garlic, minced
½ tsp. salt
½ tsp. oregano leaves, crushed
¼ tsp. ground cumin
1 can (8 oz.) tomato sauce
Dairy sour cream, chopped green onion, pitted ripe olives

Heat . . . . . . oil, ¼ inch deep, in large skillet.
Fry . . . . tortillas, one at a time, about 15 seconds on each side.
Roll . . . . into 1¾ inch wide tubes. (Wrap around rolling pin to shape if desired.) Place seam-side down on rack to cool.
Combine . . . cheese, wheat germ, ½ cup sour cream, ½ cup green onion, ½ cup ripe olives, chilies, garlic, and seasonings. Mix well.
Spoon . . . . . filling into tortilla tubes. Place seam-side down in baking dish.
Pour . . . . . . tomato sauce in wide strip down center of tortillas.
Bake . . . . . . at 350° for 20 minutes until thoroughly heated.
Spoon . . . . . additional sour cream in narrow strip on top of tomato sauce. Garnish with green onion and ripe olives.

Makes 4 flautas

ORTEGA.

Flautas with Pork Filling

1 lb. boneless pork shoulder, cut in ½ inch cubes
¼ cup chopped fresh onion
1 can (4 oz.) **ORTEGA Diced Green Chiles**
1 can (7 oz.) **ORTEGA Green Chile Salsa**
½ oz. unsweetened chocolate
¼ teaspoon salt
½ cup water
¼ cup sliced almonds
12 corn tortillas, warmed

In skillet, brown pork. Add onion. Cook until tender. Add remaining ingredients except almonds and tortillas. Stir until chocolate is melted. Simmer, uncovered, 10-15 minutes or until pork is tender and mixture is desired consistency. Mix in almonds. Lay two tortillas flat and overlapping. Spoon filling down center. Roll into long tube. Flautas may be fried in ½ inch hot (400°F) oil, if desired. Secure with toothpicks or hold together with tongs. Fry until golden but not too crisp. Garnish with salsa and sour cream, if desired.

Makes 6 flautas

Enchiladas

Mazola.

Beef Enchiladas

Refried Beans*
Enchilada Sauce**
½ pound ground beef chuck
2 teaspoons chili powder
4 tablespoons (about) **MAZOLA® Corn Oil**
8 (7-inch) corn or flour tortillas
3 tablespoons **ARGO®/KINGSFORD'S® Corn Starch**
½ teaspoon salt
⅛ teaspoon pepper
2 cups skim milk
2 ounces Monterey Jack cheese, shredded (½ cup)

Prepare Refried Beans and Enchilada Sauce. In large skillet brown beef with chili powder over medium-high heat 5 minutes or until beef loses its pink color. Drain well. Stir in refried beans. In medium skillet heat 2 tablespoons of the corn oil over medium heat. Add tortillas, one at a time. Cook 10 seconds, turning once, or until limp (do not fry until firm or crisp). Drain on paper towels. Add additional corn oil as needed. Immediately dip tortillas, one at a time, in Enchilada Sauce to soften. Place about ⅓ cup beef mixture on each tortilla; roll up and place, seam side down, in 13 x 9 x 2-inch baking dish. In 2-quart saucepan stir together corn starch, salt and pepper. Gradually stir in milk until smooth. Stir in remaining Enchilada Sauce (about 2½ cups). Stirring constantly, bring to a boil over medium heat and boil 1 minute. Pour over enchiladas. Sprinkle with cheese. Bake in 350°F oven 20 to 25 minutes or until bubbly.

Makes 8

*Refried Beans

½ pound dry pinto beans (1¼ cups)
3 cups water
2 tablespoons **MAZOLA® Corn Oil**
1 clove garlic, minced or pressed
½ teaspoon salt

In covered 2-quart saucepan bring beans and water to boil. Reduce heat to low. Simmer 2 to 2½ hours or until beans are very tender. (If necessary during cooking, add ½ to 1 cup boiling water to beans. There should be about 1 cup liquid after cooking.) In large skillet heat corn oil over medium heat. Add beans and liquid, garlic and salt. Mash beans completely. Stirring frequently, cook about 5 minutes or until mixture is very thick.

Makes about 2 cups

Note: Recipe may be doubled. Simmer beans 2½ to 3 hours.

**Enchilada Sauce

In large skillet heat 2 tablespoons **MAZOLA® Corn Oil** over medium heat. Add 1 cup chopped onion and 1 clove garlic, minced or pressed. Stirring frequently, cook 3 minutes or until tender. Stir in 1 can (16 oz.) tomatoes, undrained, chopped, 1 can (8 oz.) tomato sauce, 1 can (4 oz.) hot green chiles, drained, chopped, 1½ teaspoons chili powder and ½ teaspoon salt. Bring to boil. Reduce heat and simmer 10 to 15 minutes.

Makes about 3 cups

Ground Beef Enchiladas

1 pound lean ground beef
½ cup chopped onion
1 can (8¼ ounces) refried beans
1 can (10 ounces) enchilada sauce
2 teaspoons **KITCHEN BOUQUET®**
1½ teaspoons oregano, crumbled
½ teaspoon salt
4 full shakes **TABASCO®** or to taste
4 flour tortillas
½ cup grated Cheddar cheese

Sauté beef and onion in skillet over high heat for 5 minutes or until beef is cooked. Mix in beans, 2 tablespoons enchilada sauce, **KITCHEN BOUQUET®**, oregano, salt and **TABASCO®**. Remove from heat. Dip tortillas into some of the remaining enchilada sauce. Divide beef mixture evenly onto tortillas. Roll to enclose filling. Place seam-side down in 2-quart baking dish. Pour any remaining enchilada sauce over top. Sprinkle with cheese. Cover with lid or foil. Bake in a 350° oven for 15 minutes or until heated through. Dollop with sour cream and sprinkle with minced parsley if desired. Cooking time: 20 minutes.   *Makes 4 servings*

Health Valley® Enchiladas

2 15-ounce cans **HEALTH VALLEY® Tomato Sauce**
¾ cup water
3 teaspoons chili powder
1 clove garlic, minced
½ teaspoon turmeric
Dash of cayenne
2 15-ounce cans **HEALTH VALLEY® Spicy Vegetarian Chili With Beans**
1 12-ounce package **HEALTH VALLEY® Raw Milk Sharp Cheddar Cheese**, shredded
1 teaspoon **HEALTH VALLEY® BEST BLEND Oil**
10 **HEALTH VALLEY® Corn Tortillas**, thawed
½ cup sliced ripe olives
2 green onions, chopped

Preheat oven to 375°F. and oil an 8 × 11½-inch casserole.

In a saucepan, simmer tomato sauce, water and seasonings for 20 minutes.

Combine chili, 3 cups of cheese and ½ cup of sauce. Spoon ¼ cup sauce into prepared casserole. Soften tortillas one at a time by dipping in and out of the remaining sauce. Spoon chili-cheese mixture down center of each tortilla. Roll up and place seam side down in baking dish. Pour remaining sauce over top. Sprinkle remaining cheese, olives and green onions on top. Bake for 20 minutes in preheated oven—until hot and bubbly.

Serve with fresh avocado slices, or top the enchiladas with **HEALTH VALLEY® Avocado Dressing**. Total Preparation Time: 45 minutes.   *Yield: 5 or 6 servings*

Enchilada Bake

1 lg. can tomato sauce
1-2 tsp. garlic powder
1 tsp. onion powder
4 Tbsp. chili powder
¼ tsp. oregano
¼ tsp. basil
14 oz. **MU TOFU**
½ lb. Cheddar cheese
8-10 corn tortillas

Mix first six ingredients in saucepan. Simmer 15 min. While it's simmering grate ½ lb. Cheddar cheese, and mix into the cheese 14 oz. **MU TOFU** that has been squeezed dry.

Put ⅓ of the tomato sauce in a baking dish. Place a strip of cheese-tofu filling in each tortilla, roll them up and place in the dish. Cover with the rest of the sauce. Top with grated cheese and bake 15-20 min. at 350°.

Wiener Enchilada Casserole

OSCAR MAYER Lard
10 tortillas
1 package (1 lb.) **OSCAR MAYER Wieners**
1 can (15 oz.) enchilada sauce
1 can (6 oz.) tomato paste
½ cup finely chopped onion
½ cup (2 oz.) shredded Cheddar cheese

Preheat oven to 350°F. Melt lard in a skillet to a depth of ½-inch. Heat. Dip each tortilla in the hot lard (375°F) just long enough to soften, about 5 seconds. Drain on absorbent paper. Roll a tortilla around each wiener. Place one inch apart in greased 13x9x2-inch pan, lapped sides down. Combine enchilada sauce, tomato paste and onion. Pour sauce over wiener enchiladas in pan. Bake for 30 minutes. To serve, spoon sauce over top of wiener enchiladas and sprinkle with cheese.   *Makes 5 servings*

La Sauce™

Chicken Enchiladas

1 jar **LA SAUCE® Chicken Baking Sauce—Mild Mexican Style**
1 cup finely chopped or shredded cooked chicken
1 cup (4 oz.) shredded Cheddar cheese
⅓ cup dairy sour cream
8 corn tortillas*
Vegetable oil, heated
½ cup (2 oz.) shredded Monterey Jack cheese

Combine ⅓ cup **LA SAUCE®**, chicken, ½ cup Cheddar cheese and sour cream; set aside. In fry pan, lightly fry tortillas on medium-high heat in oil, one at a time, until soft; drain. While still hot, fill each tortilla with ⅛ chicken mixture; roll. Spread ⅓ cup **LA SAUCE®** on bottom of 12 x 8-inch baking dish. Place each rolled tortilla, seam side down, in baking dish. Spread remaining **LA SAUCE®** on top. Bake, covered with foil, at 350°, 45 minutes. Remove from oven; sprinkle remaining ½ cup Cheddar and Monterey Jack cheeses on top. Continue baking at 350°, uncovered, 5 minutes or until cheese melts.   *4 servings*

*For saucier enchiladas, use 6 tortillas.

Cheesy Chicken Enchiladas

2 Tbsp. butter or margarine
1 medium onion, chopped
1 clove garlic, minced
1 cup **KAUKAUNA® Cheese Toasted Onion Buttery Spread™**, divided
2 cups diced, cooked chicken
½ cup dairy sour cream
1 can (4 oz.) diced green chilies, drained
⅛ tsp. cayenne pepper
6 (8-inch) flour tortillas
1 can (8 oz.) tomato sauce

Melt . . . . . . butter in small skillet. Sauté onion and garlic over medium heat for 2 minutes.
Reduce . . . . heat to low. Stir in ½ cup cheese until melted.
Combine . . . cheese mixture, chicken, sour cream, chilies and cayenne pepper. Mix well.
Divide . . . . . mixture evenly on tortillas.
Roll . . . . tortillas around filling. Place seam-side-down in 13x9-inch baking dish.
Pour . . . . . . tomato sauce over tortillas.
Dollop . . . . . remaining cheese over sauce.
Bake . . . . . . covered, at 350° for 20 minutes. Uncover and bake 10 minutes longer until thoroughly heated.

Makes 6 enchiladas

Lipton.

California Enchiladas

1 can (15 oz.) tomato sauce
1 clove garlic, finely chopped
1½ teaspoons hot pepper sauce
½ pound Monterey Jack or Muenster cheese
1½ cups cut-up cooked chicken
1 cup **LIPTON® California Dip***
1 can (4 oz.) green chilies, drained and chopped
12 tortillas, softened
1 large green pepper, cut into 12 thin strips

Preheat oven to 375°. In small saucepan, combine tomato sauce, garlic and ½ teaspoon hot pepper sauce; simmer 15 minutes.

Cut cheese into 12 strips (4 x ¾ x ¼ inch) and reserve; shred remaining cheese (should equal about ½ to ¾ cup).

In large bowl, combine shredded cheese, chicken, California Dip, chilies, and remaining hot sauce. Place 2½ tablespoons mixture on each tortilla; roll up and place seam-side down in greased 2-quart oblong baking dish. Top each tortilla with 1 tablespoon prepared sauce, a cheese strip, and a green pepper strip. Bake 15 minutes or until cheese is melted. Serve with remaining sauce. *Makes 4 to 6 servings*

*Lipton® California Dip

Blend 1 envelope **LIPTON® Onion Soup Mix** with 1 pint (16 oz.) sour cream; chill. *Makes about 2 cups dip*

Shrimp Enchiladas

Heat 1 tablespoon each of butter, grated onion and flour and 2 sliced medium mushrooms until mixture bubbles. Add 1 cup sour cream and blend until warm. Mix ½ of sauce with 6 ounces thawed **BRILLIANT Cooked Shrimp**, spoon equally onto 6 tortillas and roll. Place in single layer, seam side down in shallow pan and top with remaining sauce, and thin slices of Muenster cheese. Broil for 2 minutes. *Serves 3*

Crab Enchiladas

1 pound crab meat, fresh or pasteurized
1 cup chopped onion
2 tablespoons cooking oil
1 can (10 ounces) tomatoes and green chilies
1 can (8 ounces) tomato sauce
½ cup water
½ teaspoon chili powder
½ teaspoon oregano
¼ teaspoon salt
1½ cups shredded Monterey Jack or Cheddar cheese
⅓ cup chopped pitted ripe olives
12 corn tortillas
Cooking oil for frying tortillas
Dairy sour cream (optional)

Remove any pieces of shell or cartilage from crab meat. Cook onion in oil until tender, but not brown. Add tomatoes and green chilies, tomato sauce, water, chili powder, oregano, and salt; mix well. Bring to a boil. Cover and simmer about 15 minutes to blend flavors. Combine crab meat, ½ of the cheese, olives, and ½ cup of sauce; mix. Fry tortillas, one at a time, in shallow medium-hot oil just until they are limp and begin to blister. Remove from pan and drain. Dip one tortilla at a time into remaining hot sauce. Lay flat on baking sheet. Fill each with about ¼ cup of crab meat mixture. Roll up; place flap edge down in shallow 2-quart baking dish. Spoon remaining sauce over top and sprinkle with remaining cheese. Bake in moderate oven, 350°F., 20-25 minutes or until hot. Serve topped with sour cream, if desired. *Makes 6 servings*

Favorite recipe from **Florida Department of Natural Resources**

Tuna Enchiladas del Mar

1 cup oil
12 corn tortillas
30 ounces enchilada sauce
1 12½ or 13 ounce can **CHICKEN OF THE SEA® Tuna**, drained and flaked
1 cup scallions, minced
½ pound grated Monterey Jack cheese

Preheat oven to 350°. Place oil in skillet, heat until hot. Quickly fry 12 tortillas in oil one at a time, until soft (about 4 seconds to a side).

Remove from oil and drain on paper towels. When ready to assemble the enchiladas, dip each tortilla in enchilada sauce. Place 1 tablespoon flaked tuna in center of tortilla, add 1 generous tablespoon cheese, scallions and 2 tablespoons enchilada sauce.

Roll enchiladas and place seam side down in a greased 9 × 12 baking dish. Top with remaining enchilada sauce, sprinkle with remaining cheese and bake at 350° for 20 minutes.

Garnish with sour cream, black olives, avocado slices and tomato wedges. Serve at once.

Serves 6 (2 enchiladas per serving)

Burritos

Wheat Germ Veggie Burritos

3 medium zucchini, chopped
1 can (4 oz.) chopped green chilies
½ cup finely chopped onion
1 clove garlic, minced
1 tsp. basil leaves, crushed
½ tsp. oregano leaves, crushed
¼ tsp. ground cumin
¼ tsp. salt
1 Tbsp. cooking oil
1 cup grated Monterey Jack cheese
¾ cup **KRETSCHMER Regular Wheat Germ**
8 flour tortillas
Cooking oil
Dairy sour cream
Minced parsley

Cook . . . . . . zucchini, chilies, onion, garlic and seasonings in 1 tablespoon oil over medium heat for about 5 minutes.

Add . . . . cheese and wheat germ, stirring until cheese melts. Remove from heat.

Spoon . . . . . about ½ cup vegetable mixture onto each tortilla. Roll to enclose filling.

Heat . . . . . . oil, ¼ inch deep, in large skillet. Fry burritos about 3 minutes, turning once, until golden.

Top . . . . with sour cream and parsley if desired.   *8 burritos*

Burritos

Heat:

   1 15 oz. can refried beans
   8 AZTECA® Large Flour Tortillas *or* **5 AZTECA® Super Size Flour Tortillas** (following package directions)

Place ¼ cup refried beans on one side of each tortilla, near edge. Fold in sides and roll. Serve immediately with lettuce, cheese, hot sauce as desired.

Meat Burritos

Use 2 Tbsp. beans and 2 Tbsp. Basic Meat Filling.*

*Basic Meat Filling

Fry:

   1 lb. ground beef
   ½ cup chopped onion

When meat is brown and crumbly, drain off grease.
Stir in:

   ½ cup tomato sauce
   1½ tsp. chili powder
   1 tsp. garlic powder
   ¼ tsp. pepper
   ¼ tsp. cumin

Cook until liquid is absorbed, about 10 minutes.

Smothered Burrito

1 pkg. flour tortillas
1 med. can refried beans
1 can **STOKES® Green Chile Sauce with Pork**
3 cups grated cheese (longhorn or Monterrey Jack)

Slightly warm six flour tortillas which have been lightly spread with margarine on one side. Spread a layer of refried beans on each tortilla; sprinkle cheese over beans. Roll tortilla from one side and close ends while rolling. Place burritos in pan, cover tightly with foil and heat for 20 min. in 350° oven. Remove foil, place on plate and smother with ⅓ cup preheated **STOKES® Green Chile Sauce with Pork**. Surround with thinly shredded lettuce and diced tomatoes. Serve immediately.

Makes approximately 6 smothered burritos

Tacos

A.1. Tacos

1 package (4 oz.) **ORTEGA Taco Shells**
Taco filling (recipes follow)
1 cup (4 oz.) shredded mild Cheddar cheese (or your favorite cheese)
1 cup shredded lettuce
2 medium tomatoes, diced

Warm taco shells according to package directions. Prepare taco filling. In each taco shell, place 2 tablespoons filling, 1½ tablespoons cheese, 1½ tablespoons lettuce, and 1 tablespoon tomatoes. Top with **ORTEGA Taco Sauce**, if desired. Serve immediately.   *Serves 4-6*

Tex-Mex Taco Filling

1 lb. ground beef
1 medium onion, chopped
1 medium clove garlic, minced
3 tablespoons **A.1. Steak Sauce**
1 can (8 oz.) tomato sauce
2 teaspoons chili powder
½ teaspoon salt

In skillet, brown beef until crumbly. Drain. Add onion and garlic. Cook until onion is soft. Add remaining ingredients. Simmer, uncovered, 10 minutes, stirring occasionally.

Makes filling for 10 tacos

Yankee Taco Filling

1 lb. ground beef
1 medium onion, chopped
1 medium clove garlic, minced
3 tablespoons **A.1. Steak Sauce**
½ cup (2 oz.) shredded sharp Cheddar cheese

In skillet, brown beef until crumbly. Drain. Add onion and garlic. Cook until onion is soft. Stir in **A.1.** and cheese. Heat until cheese is melted.   *Makes filling for 10 tacos*

Tac-Oats

1 lb. ground beef
½ cup chopped onion
8 oz. bottle taco sauce
½ cup 3-MINUTE BRAND® Oats
3½ oz. can sliced black olives, drained
½ tsp. salt
½ tsp. garlic salt
½-1 cup water
8 to 10 taco shells
1 cup chopped tomato
1 cup chopped avocado
1 cup shredded longhorn/Cheddar cheese
1 cup finely shredded lettuce

Brown beef and onions in a deep skillet, crumbling meat as it cooks. Drain excess fat. Add taco sauce, oats, olives, salt and garlic salt. Cover and simmer over low heat for 20 minutes, adding water as mixture appears dry. Heat taco shells in oven. When hot, spoon filling into them. Sprinkle each with tomato, avocado, cheese and lettuce. Serve hot.

Mexicali Tacos

2 pounds ground beef
½ cup chopped green pepper
1 can (11¼ ounces) CAMPBELL'S Condensed Chili
    Beef Soup
1 can (10¾ ounces) CAMPBELL'S Condensed
    Tomato Soup
1 to 2 tablespoons finely chopped cherry peppers
24 taco shells
Shredded Cheddar or Monterey Jack cheese
Shredded lettuce
Chopped onion
Chopped tomato

In skillet, brown beef and cook green pepper until tender; stir to separate meat. Add soups and cherry peppers. Cook over low heat 5 minutes; stir occasionally. Fill each taco shell with 3 to 4 tablespoons meat mixture; top with remaining ingredients.

Makes 24 tacos

Gerber®

Tacos

2 tablespoons onion
2 tablespoons celery
1 tablespoon margarine
4 jars (3½ oz. each) GERBER® Junior Beef
1 can (15½ oz.) refried beans
½ cup chopped tomato
3 tablespoons quick rice
1 teaspoon chili powder
½ teaspoon salt
¼ teaspoon garlic powder
Dash hot pepper sauce
16 taco shells
Garnishes for tacos: olives, shredded cheese, chopped
    onions, green pepper, etc.

In a skillet, brown onion and celery in margarine; mix in beef, refried beans, and chopped tomato. Add remaining ingredients, stir until well mixed. Bring to a boil, reduce heat, and simmer for 10 minutes.

Spoon taco meat filling into taco shells; add garnishes and serve immediately.   *Yield: 16*

Green Chile Turkey Tacos

Cranberry Salsa:
1 medium onion, chopped
1 small clove garlic, minced
1 tablespoon cooking oil
1 cup OCEAN SPRAY® Cranberry Orange Sauce
¼ cup canned, diced, mild green chile
2 tablespoons red wine vinegar
½ teaspoon salt

Turkey Filling:
1 small onion, chopped
1 tablespoon oil
1 teaspoon cornstarch
½ cup turkey or chicken broth
1½ cups shredded cooked turkey
1 tablespoon canned, diced, mild green chile
Salt to taste

To Assemble Tacos:
8 packaged taco shells
Shredded iceberg lettuce

PREPARE SALSA:
In small saucepan, cook onion and garlic in hot oil until tender. Stir in cranberry orange sauce, chile, vinegar and salt. Cover. Refrigerate until cold.

PREPARE FILLING:
In medium saucepan, cook onion in oil until tender. Stir in cornstarch then broth. Heat to boiling. Stir in turkey and chile. Add salt to taste; keep filling warm.

TO ASSEMBLE:
Place taco shells on a baking sheet and heat in a 250°F oven for 10 minutes. Spoon 2 to 3 tablespoons turkey mixture into each heated shell. Top with some shredded lettuce and serve with salsa.

Makes 4 servings

Chicken Tacos

1 jar LA SAUCE® Chicken Baking Sauce—Mild
    Mexican Style
2 cups chopped or shredded cooked chicken
8 taco shells, heated
½ head lettuce, shredded
1 cup chopped tomato
1 cup (4 oz.) shredded Cheddar cheese

In saucepan, combine LA SAUCE® and chicken; cook on low heat 10 minutes. Spoon chicken mixture into taco shells; top with lettuce, tomato and cheese.   *8 tacos*

Spicy Tacos

1 can (12½ oz.) **BUMBLE BEE® Chunk Light
  Tuna***
½ cup dairy sour cream
1 can (4 oz.) diced green chiles
½ teaspoon ground cumin
6 taco shells
1 avocado, seeded, peeled and sliced
1 tomato, diced
1 stalk green onion, chopped

Drain tuna. Combine tuna, sour cream, green chiles and cumin. Spoon tuna mixture into each taco shell. Add avocado slices and tomatoes. Garnish with green onion.   *Makes 6 servings*

*Or use 2 cans (6½ oz. each) **BUMBLE BEE® Chunk Light
Tuna**.

Tacos Alchili

Heat mixture of equal parts **WOLF® Brand Chili** and refried beans, spoon into taco shell. Cover with lettuce, tomato, and grated cheese. Add picante sauce.

Tostadas

Acapulco
Tostada

1 tablespoon vegetable oil
½ pound lean ground beef
½ cup chopped onion
1 clove garlic, pressed
2 teaspoons chili powder
¼ teaspoon salt
1 green-tipped, medium **DOLE® Banana**
2 corn tortillas
Vegetable oil for frying
1½ cups shredded iceberg lettuce
1 small tomato, thinly sliced
½ cup shredded Cheddar cheese
2 tablespoons dairy sour cream

Heat oil in 10-inch skillet. Add beef, onion, garlic, chili powder and salt. Sauté about 5 minutes, just until meat is no longer pink. Peel banana; halve lengthwise and slice to make small cubes. Add to meat mixture and cook until heated, about 1 minute. Drain

excess fat from meat; keep meat warm. In separate skillet, fry tortillas in oil until crisp; place each on individual serving plate. Add lettuce and cover with meat mixture. Top with tomato and cheese. Garnish each with a tablespoon sour cream.
Makes 2 servings

Tas-Tee Tostadas

6 tortillas
2 avocados, peeled, pitted and mashed
¼ cup **HENRI'S TAS-TEE® Dressing**
¼ cup finely chopped onion
⅛ teaspoon hot pepper sauce
1½ cups shredded lettuce
12 thin slices roast beef
3 medium tomatoes, chopped
1 cup grated mild Cheddar cheese
Chili powder or taco sauce

1. Fry tortillas in hot oil until crisp and lightly browned. Drain. Set aside.
2. Combine avocados, **HENRI'S TAS-TEE® Dressing,** onion and hot pepper sauce. Mix well.
3. Spread each crisp tortilla with the avocado-**HENRI'S TAS-TEE® Dressing** mixture.
4. Top with lettuce, beef slices, chopped tomato and cheese.
5. Sprinkle with chili powder or taco sauce to taste.
Makes 6 tostadas

Tostadas
with Pork

1 pound ground lean pork
1 cup chopped onion
1 jar (8 ounces) taco sauce
1 teaspoon salt
½ teaspoon chili powder
¼ cup sliced pitted ripe olives
Cooking oil
4 corn or flour tortillas, about 7-inch diameter
3 to 4 cups shredded lettuce
½ cup shredded Monterey Jack or Cheddar cheese,
  optional
1 medium-size tomato, cut in thin wedges
½ cup dairy sour cream
Additional taco sauce, optional

In skillet, lightly brown ground pork and onion. Add taco sauce, salt and chili powder; cover and cook over low heat 15 minutes or until pork is done and flavors blended. Stir in ripe olives. Heat about ⅛ inch oil in large skillet over medium high heat. Fry tortillas, one at a time, turning frequently until crisp, slightly puffed and lightly browned. Drain on paper towels. For each tostada place a crisp tortilla on a plate. Top with layer of lettuce, then hot pork mixture (about ⅔ cup). Sprinkle with cheese, if used. Garnish with tomato wedges and dollop of sour cream. Serve with additional taco sauce, if desired.
Makes 4 large tostadas

Note: If large tortillas are not available, make 6 to 8 tostadas using the smaller tortillas.

Favorite recipe from **National Pork Producers Council**

Egg Tostados

12 tostado shells
1 to 2 cans (16 oz. each) refried beans
1 cup chopped onion
1 cup chopped green pepper
1 cup chopped tomato
¼ cup butter
12 eggs
1 cup (4 oz.) shredded Cheddar cheese
Taco sauce

Place tostado shells on cookie sheets and heat in preheated 350°F. oven 5 to 10 minutes, or until crisp. Meanwhile in saucepan cook beans over medium heat until hot, stirring occasionally. Spread beans over tostado shells. Sprinkle each tostado with about 1 tablespoon each chopped onion, green pepper and tomato. Heat butter in large fry pan until just hot enough to sizzle a drop of water. Break and slip eggs into fry pan. Reduce heat immediately. Cook slightly under desired degree of doneness, spooning butter over eggs to baste or turning eggs to cook both sides. Place 1 egg on each tostado. Sprinkle with about 1 tablespoon cheese. Broil 4 to 6 inches from heat just until cheese melts. Serve hot with taco sauce.   *6 servings*

Favorite recipe from the **American Egg Board**

Meat

Mexican Liver

6 slices bacon
¾ cup onions, chopped
1 clove garlic, minced
¼ cup flour
1½ teaspoons chili powder
1 teaspoon salt
1½ lb. liver, cut in thin strips
1 can (16 oz.) **FURMAN'S® Whole Tomatoes**
1 can (16 oz.) **FURMAN'S® Whole Kernel Corn**, drained
Hot cooked rice

In large skillet cook bacon until crisp. Reserve 3 tablespoons drippings in skillet. Crumble bacon and set aside. Cook onions and garlic in drippings until onions are tender but not brown, about 5 minutes. Combine flour, chili powder and salt. Cut liver into thin strips, toss in flour mixture to coat. Add liver to onions and brown quickly on all sides. Stir in bacon, undrained tomatoes and corn. Simmer covered until mixture is heated through. Serve over cooked rice.   *Serves 6*

Straw Hats

1 can **ELLIS® Chili No Beans** or **Chili with Beans**
1 can **ELLIS® Tamales**
4 oz. longhorn cheese—grated
⅓ cup sour cream
½ cup guacamole—optional

Heat **ELLIS® Chili** and **ELLIS® Tamales** in separate containers. Place two tamales on each plate, smother with 5 oz. of chili and sprinkle cheese over top. Melt cheese under broiler or in microwave. Add a dab of sour cream and guacamole for color.   *3 servings*

Rio Grande Franks

1 medium avocado, diced
2 teaspoons lemon juice
1 (8-ounce) can tomato sauce or puree
1 cup beer or tomato juice
1 medium onion, chopped
1 to 1½ teaspoons chili powder
1 cup shredded hot pepper cheese (4 ounces)
1 pound wieners, slashed
4 or 5 (6-or-8-inch) flour tortillas
Sour cream

In small bowl toss avocado with lemon juice. Set aside. In 5-quart pot combine tomato sauce, beer, onion and chili powder. Bring to boiling. Reduce heat and stir in cheese. Cook and stir over low heat until cheese melts. Cover sauce and keep warm. Broil or grill wieners 5 inches from heat for about 5 minutes or until of desired doneness. Place 2 wieners on each tortilla. Spoon on sauce, using about ⅓ cup for each serving. Top with sour cream and avocado.   *Makes 4 or 5 servings*

Favorite recipe from **National Hot Dog & Sausage Council**

Mexican Lamb

6 lamb shanks
1½ teaspoons salt
1 teaspoon pepper
½ teaspoon garlic powder
1 large onion, chopped
2 cups milk
3 jars (8-oz.) junior peaches
4 teaspoons **ANGOSTURA® Aromatic Bitters**
½ teaspoon marjoram
Pinch thyme
¼ teaspoon rosemary
⅓ cup raisins
Cooked rice
Cling peach slices

Rub lamb shanks with salt, pepper and garlic powder. Place in large pan, cover with boiling water and simmer until almost tender, about 45 minutes. Remove shanks and trim off meat, discarding bones. Cut meat into bite-size pieces. Place lamb in large skillet and add onion and milk. Simmer all together gently until the milk is almost absorbed. Add junior peaches, **ANGOSTURA® Aromatic Bitters**, marjoram, thyme, rosemary and raisins. Heat together slowly, stirring occasionally, for about 20 minutes. To serve, arrange hot cooked rice on large platter, spoon meat mixture over top, and garnish with peach slices.   *Yield: 6 servings*

Spaghetti Mexicali

For every pound of dry spaghetti used, heat up 20 ounces of **JAMES RIVER SMITHFIELD Chili Sauce**; pour over cooked spaghetti and serve.

South of the Border Style

¼ cup chopped onion
¼ cup chopped green pepper
1 tablespoon butter or margarine
2 15-ounce cans (4 cups) **BROADCAST® Chili with Beans**
1 12-ounce can (1½ cups) whole kernel corn, drained
1 4½-ounce can (¾ cup) chopped ripe olives
1 4-ounce package (1 cup) shredded sharp Cheddar cheese
1 package corn muffin mix

In large skillet, cook onion, and pepper in butter till tender. Stir in chili, corn, and olives; bring to boiling. Add cheese; stir to melt. Pour into 11 x 7 x 1½-inch baking pan.

Prepare muffin mix according to package directions. Spoon dough in diagonal bands across top of casserole; (bake any remaining dough in muffin pans and freeze for later use). Bake at 400° for 15 to 20 minutes.   *Serves 8*

Frankly Mexican Casserole

1 package **FRENCH'S® Scalloped Potatoes**
½ pound frankfurters, sliced
1 can (15-oz.) kidney beans, drained and rinsed
1 tablespoon butter or margarine
¼ cup fine dry bread crumbs
½ teaspoon **FRENCH'S® Chili Powder**

Prepare potatoes as directed on package, except use 2-quart casserole and increase boiling water to 2⅔ cups. Stir in frankfurters and beans. Bake in 400° oven 35 minutes; stir casserole. Melt butter in small pan; stir in bread crumbs and chili powder. Sprinkle over casserole and bake 10 to 15 minutes longer, until potatoes are tender.   *6 servings*

MICROWAVE METHOD:
Combine potato slices with 3 cups hot tap water in 2-quart casserole. Cover; cook on HIGH 14 minutes. Stir in ⅔ cup milk, seasoning mix, kidney beans, and frankfurters. Cook, covered, 7 minutes. Sprinkle with crumb mixture; cook 2 minutes.

Chilli Man® Taco Casserole

1 package (approx. 6 oz.) corn chips
1 can (20 oz.) **CHILLI MAN® Chilli with Beans**
1 can (16 oz.) stewed tomatoes
1 jalapeño pepper, chopped (optional)
½ cup sliced black olives, optional
1 cup (4 oz.) shredded cheese (brick, Cheddar, etc.)

Crush half the corn chips and line an 8-inch casserole dish. Add: layer of Chilli, spoon over the tomatoes, sprinkle with olives and jalapeño pepper, top with remaining chips and cheese. Bake in 350° oven about 30 minutes or until bubbly and brown.

Makes about 8 servings

Beef

Mexican Beef Casserole

1 (7-ounce) package or 2 cups uncooked **CREAMETTES® Elbow Macaroni,** cooked as package directs and drained
1 pound lean ground beef
¾ cup chopped green pepper
¾ cup chopped onion
1 clove garlic, finely chopped
2 cups hot water
1 (16-ounce) can tomatoes, cut up and undrained
1 (6-ounce) can tomato paste
1 (12-ounce) can whole kernel corn, drained
¼ cup pitted ripe olives, sliced if desired
1 (8-ounce) can tomato sauce
2 teaspoons chili powder
1 teaspoon oregano leaves
1 teaspoon salt
⅛ teaspoon ground cumin, optional
Corn chips
½ cup (2 ounces) shredded Cheddar cheese

Preheat oven to 350°. In large skillet, brown meat; pour off fat. Add green pepper, onion and garlic; cook and stir until tender. Stir in cooked macaroni, water, tomatoes, tomato paste, corn and olives. Pour into 3-quart shallow baking dish (13x9-inch). Stir together tomato sauce and seasonings; pour over macaroni mixture. Bake 25 to 30 minutes or until hot; top with corn chips and cheese. Bake 5 minutes longer or until cheese melts. Refrigerate leftovers.   *Makes 8 servings*

Rio Grande Stew

2 pounds beef cubes for stew
Flour
¼ cup vegetable oil
4½ cups water
1 (16-ounce) can stewed tomatoes, undrained
2 medium onions, cut into wedges
7 teaspoons **WYLER'S® Beef-Flavor Instant Bouillon** *or* 7 Beef-Flavor Bouillon Cubes
1 teaspoon ground coriander, optional
1 teaspoon ground cumin
1 teaspoon oregano leaves
¼ teaspoon garlic powder
1 bay leaf
1 cup sliced carrots
2 ears fresh or thawed frozen corn, cut into chunks
1 small head cabbage, cut into wedges (about 1 pound)
1 (4-ounce) can chopped mild green chilies, drained

In paper or plastic bag, add meat, a few pieces at a time, to flour; shake to coat. In Dutch oven, brown meat in oil. Add remaining ingredients except carrots, corn, cabbage and chilies. Bring to a boil. Reduce heat; cover and simmer 1½ hours. Add remaining ingredients; cook 30 minutes longer or until vegetables are tender. Remove bay leaf. Refrigerate leftovers.   *Makes 8 servings*

Elam's®
Elam's® Tamale Pie

1½ cups cold water
1½ cups **ELAM'S® Stone Ground 100% Whole Yellow Corn Meal**
1½ teaspoons salt
2 cups boiling water
1 pound ground beef chuck or round
½ cup chopped onion
2 tablespoons flour
1 teaspoon chili powder
1 can (1 pound) tomatoes
1 can (8 ounces) tomato sauce
1 can (8¾ ounces) whole kernel corn, drained (1 cup)

Combine and mix cold water and corn meal. Add ½ teaspoon salt to boiling water. Add corn meal mixture, stirring constantly, bring to a boil. Partially cover pan; cook slowly 7 minutes, stirring often. Line bottom and sides of greased 2-quart casserole with cooked mush. Cook beef and onion in fry pan until beef is grey and crumbly. Stir in flour, remaining 1 teaspoon salt and chili powder. Add tomatoes, breaking them up into chunks with spoon. Stir in tomato sauce and corn. Spoon into mush-lined casserole. Bake in moderate oven (350°F) until hot and bubbly, 40 to 45 minutes.   *Yield: 6 servings*

Van Camp's® Mexican Pie

1¼ cups biscuit mix
¼ cup commercial sour cream
1 egg, beaten
1 pound lean ground beef
1 teaspoon salt
½ cup chopped onion
1 can (15½ ounces) **VAN CAMP'S® Mexican Style Chili Beans**
½ cup shredded lettuce
1 cup diced fresh tomato
¾ cup grated Monterey Jack cheese

Preheat oven to 425°F. Combine biscuit mix, sour cream, and egg. Mix to form soft dough. With lightly floured hands, spread dough on bottom and up sides of greased 10 x 6 x 1¾-inch pan. Brown ground beef; drain excess fat. Add salt, onion, and chili beans; mix well and spoon into crust. Bake 20 to 30 minutes, or until edge of crust is deep golden brown. Top with lettuce, tomato, and cheese. Let stand 5 minutes before cutting.   *6 servings*

SOMETHING GOOD ALWAYS COMES OF IT

Impossible Taco Pie

1 pound ground beef
1 medium onion, chopped (about ½ cup)
1 envelope (1¼ ounces) taco seasoning mix
1 can (4 ounces) chopped green chilies, drained
1¼ cups milk
3 eggs
¾ cup **BISQUICK® Baking Mix**
2 tomatoes, sliced
1 cup shredded Monterey Jack or Cheddar cheese (4 ounces)

Heat oven to 400°. Grease pie plate, 10 x 1½ inches. Cook and stir ground beef and onion in 10-inch skillet until beef is brown; drain. Stir in taco seasoning mix (dry). Spread in plate; sprinkle with chilies. Beat milk, eggs and baking mix until smooth, 15 seconds in blender on high or 1 minute with hand beater. Pour into plate. Bake 25 minutes. Top with tomatoes; sprinkle with cheese. Bake until cheese is golden brown and knife inserted in center comes out clean, 8 to 10 minutes longer. Cool 5 minutes. Serve with sour cream, chopped tomatoes and shredded lettuce if desired.
6 to 8 servings

Potato BUDS
Mexican Pie

BETTY CROCKER® POTATO BUDS® Mashed Potatoes (enough for 4 servings)
1 egg, slightly beaten
¼ cup sliced green onions (with tops)
2 tablespoons dairy sour cream
1 pound ground beef
1 small green pepper, chopped (about ½ cup)
1 medium onion, chopped (about ½ cup)
1 can (8 ounces) tomato sauce
¼ cup sliced pitted ripe olives
2 to 3 teaspoons chili powder
¼ teaspoon salt
1 large clove garlic, crushed
1 cup shredded Cheddar or Monterey Jack cheese (about 4 ounces)

Heat oven to 425°. Grease pie plate 9 x 1¼ inches. Prepare mashed potatoes as directed on package for 4 servings except—decrease water to 1 cup and omit milk. Stir in egg, green onions and sour cream. Press potato mixture against bottom and side of pie plate. Prick bottom and side with fork. Bake 15 minutes.

Cook and stir ground beef, green pepper and chopped onion in 10-inch skillet until beef is brown; drain. Stir in remaining ingredients except cheese. Cover and cook over low heat, stirring occasionally, 5 minutes. Spoon into pie shell; sprinkle with cheese. Bake until cheese is melted, 2 to 3 minutes.
4 or 5 servings

Rosarita®

Chili Casserole

1 pound ground beef
½ cup chopped onion
1 tablespoon chili powder
1 teaspoon salt
¼ teaspoon oregano
1 can (30 ounces) **ROSARITA® Refried Beans**
1 can (16 ounces) stewed tomatoes
6 ounces Monterey Jack cheese
2 cups slightly broken tortilla chips

Brown beef and onion in skillet. Add chili powder, salt and oregano. Stir in beans and tomatoes. Remove from heat. Shred cheese, reserving ½ cup for topping. Spoon ½ of beef mixture into 2-quart casserole. Sprinkle with half of cheese; top with half of tortilla chips. Repeat layers. Bake at 350° for 20 minutes. Sprinkle with reserved ½ cup of cheese. Bake 5 minutes longer or until cheese has melted and mixture is bubbly.   *8 servings*

28

Featherweight®
Spicy Baked Casserole
(Low Sodium)

1 can (8 oz.) FEATHERWEIGHT® Vegetable-Beef
  Soup
½ pound hamburger
¼ cup onion, chopped
2 Tbsp. green pepper, chopped
⅓ cup FEATHERWEIGHT® Chili Sauce
½-1 cup noodles, cooked
⅛ tsp. FEATHERWEIGHT® K-Salt
Dash pepper

Brown hamburger, add onion and green pepper. Cook a few
minutes. Stir in remaining ingredients. Pour into casserole dish.
Bake at 350° F for 30 minutes.   *Serves 3*

Taco Twirl Casserole

2 cups GIOIA® Spirals, uncooked
1 pound ground beef
1 package taco seasoning (1½ ounce)
1 cup chopped green onion
1½ cups grated Cheddar cheese
½ head shredded lettuce
1 15 ounce can kidney beans, drained
⅓ cup black olives, chopped
1 package taco flavored corn chips (5½ ounce)
½ bottle French dressing

Cook GIOIA® Spirals according to package directions, drain
well and rinse with cold water to cool. Brown meat and drain fat.
Add taco seasoning and mix well, cool.

Combine the cooled, cooked GIOIA® Spirals, green onion,
cheese, black olives, seasoned ground beef, kidney beans and
lettuce. Mix well. Before serving, stir in the French dressing, add
the taco chips. Toss lightly.   *Serves 6-8*

DANNON® YOGURT
Dannon® Mexican Beef Casserole

1 tablespoon vegetable oil
½ cup chopped onion
2 garlic cloves, minced
1 pound lean ground beef
1 28-ounce can stewed tomatoes, drained
1 package taco seasoning mix
1 4-ounce can green chiles, drained and diced
1 2½-ounce can black olives, drained and chopped
1 16-ounce package cheese-flavored tortilla chips,
  lightly crushed
½ pound mozzarella cheese, shredded
2 8-ounce or 1-16 ounce container Plain DANNON®
  Yogurt
½ cup shredded Cheddar cheese

Preheat oven to 350°. Heat oil in larg...
Sauté onion and garlic in oil until t...
until browned, stirring frequently. Ble...
ing, chiles and olives; simmer 10 mi...
baking dish. Layer half of the chip...
mixture, mozzarella and yogurt. Top...
30 minutes or until heated thorough...
cheese; bake until cheese melts. Let s...
serving.

Cookout Chuck Steak

2 beef chuck blade steaks, cut ¾-inch thick
  (approximately 4 pounds)
1 envelope LIPTON® Beefy Onion Soup Mix
½ cup dry red wine
¼ cup red wine vinegar
1 tablespoon Worcestershire sauce
1 can (8 ounces) tomato sauce
¼ cup brown sugar
1 tablespoon chili powder
¼ teaspoon cumin, if desired

Combine beefy onion soup mix, wine, vinegar, and Worcestershire sauce. Place steaks in utility dish or plastic bag; add
marinade, turning to coat steaks. Cover dish or tie bag securely
and marinate in refrigerator 6 to 8 hours (or overnight), turning at
least once. Drain marinade from meat and combine with tomato
sauce, brown sugar, chili powder and cumin, if desired, in small
saucepan; cook slowly 10 minutes, stirring occasionally. Place
steaks on grill so surface of meat is 4 inches from heat. Broil at
moderate temperature 7 to 10 minutes on each side, depending
upon degree of doneness desired (rare or medium). Brush steaks
with sauce occasionally while broiling.   *6 to 8 servings*

Favorite recipe from **Iowa Beef Industry Council**

Mexican Lasagna

1½ lb. ground beef
½ cup chopped onion
½ cup chopped celery
2 - 8 oz. cans tomato sauce
1 - 14½ oz. can stewed tomatoes, drained and chopped
1 - 4 oz. can chopped green chillies
¼ cup sliced ripe olives
1 - 1¼ oz. pkg. taco seasoning mix
2 tsp. BALTIMORE SPICE OLD BAY Seasoning
10-12 corn tortillas
8 oz. (1 cup) ricotta cheese
2 eggs, slightly beaten
9 oz. Monterey Jack, grated

In skillet, cook ground beef, onion, and celery until meat is brown
and vegetables are tender; drain. Stir in tomato sauce, tomatoes,
chillies, olives, and seasonings. Simmer, uncovered, 15 minutes.
Cut tortillas in quarters. In small bowl, combine ricotta cheese and
eggs. Spread one-half of the meat mixture in the bottom of a
13x9x2 inch baking dish. Top with one-half of the tortillas, then
one-half of the egg mixture, and one-half of the grated cheese.
Repeat the layers ending with the cheese. Bake uncovered at 350°F
for 30 minutes. Let stand 10 minutes before serving. May be
garnished with sliced ripe olives and fried tortilla quarters.

Red Star® Mexican Pizza

2½ cups all-purpose flour
1 package **RED STAR® Instant Blend Dry Yeast**
½ cup cornmeal
1 teaspoon sugar
1 teaspoon salt
1 cup warm water
2 tablespoons oil
1½ lb. lean ground beef
2 cans (7½ oz. each) taco sauce
2 cans (4 oz. each) green chilies, drained and chopped
8 ounces natural Monterey Jack cheese, sliced ⅛-inch thick
Sliced green onions
Shredded lettuce

In large mixer bowl, combine 1 cup flour, yeast, cornmeal, sugar and salt; mix well. Add water (120-130°), and oil to flour mixture. Blend at low speed until moistened; beat 3 minutes at medium speed. By hand, gradually stir in enough remaining flour to make a soft dough. Knead on floured surface, 5 to 8 minutes. Place in greased bowl, turning to grease top. Cover; let rise in warm place until double, about 45 minutes.

Prepare Topping: In large skillet, lightly brown beef; drain. Stir in taco sauce. Cook, uncovered, 5 to 10 minutes until almost dry. Remove from heat; cool.

Punch down dough. Divide into 2 parts. Shape each half into a ball; place on greased cookie sheets. Using palms of hands, pat dough into a 12-inch circle, making edges slightly thick. Spread meat mixture over dough. Arrange chilies and cheese over meat. Bake at 425° for 15 to 20 minutes until crust is golden brown. Sprinkle with onions and lettuce. Serve immediately.

Two 12-inch pizzas

Mexican Pizza

Pizza Dough*
1 pound ground beef
3 green onions (with tops), sliced
1 clove garlic, finely chopped
¼ teaspoon salt
1 can (15 ounces) refried beans
1 can (4 ounces) chopped green chilies, drained
1 jar (9 ounces) taco sauce
2 cups shredded Monterey Jack and/or Cheddar cheese (about 8 ounces)

Prepare Pizza Dough. Heat oven to 400°. Cook and stir ground beef, onions and garlic in 10-inch skillet over medium-high heat until beef is brown; drain. Sprinkle with salt. Spread refried beans to edge of pizza dough. Layer beef mixture, chilies, taco sauce and cheese on refried beans. Bake until crust is golden brown and cheese is bubbly in center, about 20 minutes. Serve with chopped tomatoes, dairy sour cream, guacamole and shredded lettuce if desired.

Note: Pizza can be prepared ahead; cover and refrigerate no longer than 4 hours. Bake about 30 minutes.

(Continued)

*Pizza Dough

1½ cups **GOLD MEDAL WONDRA® Flour**
½ cup yellow cornmeal
3 teaspoons baking powder
1 teaspoon salt
⅓ cup shortening
¾ cup milk

Mix flour, cornmeal, baking powder and salt; cut in shortening until mixture resembles fine crumbs. Stir in milk until dough forms. Turn dough onto well-floured cloth-covered board. Shape into ball; knead until smooth, 10 to 12 times. Roll into 13-inch circle; fold into quarters. Place on ungreased cookie sheet; unfold. Pinch edge of circle, forming 1-inch rim.

Deep Dish Mexican Pizza

2½ cups biscuit baking mix
½ cup yellow cornmeal
¾ cup water
1 pound lean ground beef
½ cup chopped onion
1 (8-ounce) can tomato sauce
1 (4-ounce) can chopped mild green chilies, drained
1 tablespoon **WYLER'S® Beef-Flavor Instant Bouillon** *or* 3 **Beef-Flavor Bouillon Cubes**
1 teaspoon chili powder
¼ teaspoon ground cumin
1 (16-ounce) can refried beans
1½ cups (6 ounces) shredded mild Cheddar *or* Monterey Jack cheese
Chopped tomato
Shredded lettuce
Sliced pitted ripe olives

Preheat oven to 425°. In medium bowl, combine biscuit mix, cornmeal and water; mix well. With floured hands, pat dough on bottom and up sides of greased 15x10-inch jellyroll pan. Bake 10 minutes; remove from oven. In large skillet, brown meat with onion; stir in tomato sauce, chilies, bouillon, chili powder and cumin. Cook and stir until bouillon dissolves. Spread beans evenly over baked crust; spoon meat mixture evenly over beans. Top with cheese. Bake 10 minutes. Garnish with tomato, lettuce and olives. Refrigerate leftovers. *Makes 8 to 10 servings*

Spanish Noodles

2 Tbsp. oil
1 med. onion, chopped
½ med. green pepper, chopped
½ cup chopped celery
1 lb. ground beef
2 8-oz. cans tomato sauce
2 8-oz. cans water
1 Tbsp. brown sugar
2 Tbsp. **MARUKAN® Rice Vinegar (Genuine Brewed)**
1 tsp. salt
6 oz. of noodles uncooked

Heat oil in large skillet. Sauté vegetables in skillet until golden brown and slightly transparent. Push the vegetables to one side of the skillet. Add meat and brown lightly. Add remaining ingredients and mix together. Cover. Bring the mixture to boil over full flame. Adjust to simmer and continue cooking 25 to 30 minutes.

Frijoles y Carne Monterey

1 pound ground beef
½ pound sweet Italian sausage
1 can (16-ounces) whole tomatoes
1 can (15-ounces) kidney beans, drained
1 can (8¾-ounces) corn, drained
1 package dry enchilada sauce mix
8 ARGA'S Corn Tortilla Conchas (recipe follows)
1 cup Cheddar cheese, grated

Brown ground beef and sausage in large skillet, drain. Chop whole tomatoes, add to meat mixture with kidney beans, corn, and enchilada sauce mix. Simmer for 15 minutes.

Spoon mixture into tortilla conchas and sprinkle with Cheddar cheese. Place tortilla conchas on a baking sheet and bake at 350 degrees for 20 minutes or until cheese has melted and conchas are heated through.   *Makes 8 servings*

Arga's Tortilla Conchas

1 ARGA'S (regular size) Flour or Corn Tortilla
1 soup can, empty
2 pieces (18-inches long) string
Oil

Place one warm tortilla under bottom of soup can. Take one piece of string and place it along the bottom of the can, bringing it up the sides and tying at the top.

Repeat with the second piece of string bringing it up the can on opposite sides, forming an "X" at the top of the can.

Using tongs, emerse can into oil and deep fat fry until crisp. Drain and cool slightly before removing string.
Makes 1 tortilla concha

Beef Mexicana

1 lb. lean ground beef
2 cans (8 oz. each) tomato sauce
¾ cup ROMAN MEAL® Cereal
½ cup chopped onion
2 tablespoons chopped green pepper
1 teaspoon salt
½ teaspoon pepper
1 can (16 oz.) whole kernel corn, drained
2 teaspoons chili powder

Mix beef, 1 can tomato sauce, cereal, onion, green pepper, salt and pepper. In large skillet, over medium heat, brown meat mixture, breaking apart and stirring it with a fork. Stir in the remaining can of tomato sauce, the corn and chili powder. Simmer uncovered 30 minutes, stirring occasionally. Serve over toasted burger buns or corn chips.   *Serves 5*

MICROWAVE METHOD:
Combine first 6 ingredients in a 2 or 3-quart casserole dish. Cook on full power 7 minutes; stir once. Stir in remaining ingredients. Cover and cook 10 minutes on full power; stir once.

Rio Ramen

Before opening break up noodles in a pkg. **Beef Flavor TOP RAMEN®.** Add noodles to 1 cup boiling water. Cook uncovered, stir occasionally for 3 minutes. Rinse and drain well. Cook ½ lb. ground beef with seasonings from flavor packet and ½ tsp. Mexican seasonings (or chili powder) until meat is browned. Arrange meat over hot noodles. Top with your choice of shredded cheese, shredded lettuce, taco sauce, sour cream, avocado slices.
Serves 2

Taco Crepes

Crepes:
⅔ cup uncooked Regular, Quick or Instant CREAM OF WHEAT Cereal
⅓ cup all-purpose flour
1½ cups milk
2 eggs
1 tablespoon vegetable oil
¼ teaspoon salt

Filling:
¾ pound lean ground beef
1 cup chopped onion
1 cup chopped green pepper
1 clove garlic, crushed
1 (15-ounce) can chili without beans
1 (8-ounce) can tomato sauce
½ to 1 teaspoon chili powder

Topping:
Grated Cheddar cheese
Dairy sour cream

1. **Make Crepes:** In medium bowl, combine **CREAM OF WHEAT Cereal**, flour, milk, eggs, oil and salt; beat with wire whisk until well blended. Refrigerate at least 4 hours or overnight.

2. Over high heat, heat lightly greased 6-inch skillet or crepe pan; remove from heat; stir batter well; spoon in about 2 tablespoons. Return to heat; cook 1 to 2 minutes; turn; cook 30 seconds to 1 minute longer. Stir batter and repeat until all batter is used.
Makes 14 crepes

3. **Make Filling:** Preheat oven to 375°F. In large skillet, over medium heat, brown beef, onion, green pepper and garlic, stirring occasionally, until meat is no longer pink; drain fat. Stir in chili, tomato sauce and chili powder; simmer, stirring occasionally, 5 minutes. Remove from heat.

4. Spoon about ¼ to ⅓ cup filling into center of each crepe; fold opposite edges of crepe over top, overlapping slightly to contain filling. Place seam-side down in shallow baking dish. Heat about 10 minutes or until piping hot. Serve with grated Cheddar cheese and sour cream.
Makes 14 crepes

MICROWAVE METHOD:
1. In 3-quart microwave-proof dish, microwave ground beef, onion, green pepper and garlic at 100% power 6 minutes, stirring after 3 minutes, or until meat is no longer pink and vegetables are tender. Drain fat.

2. Add remaining ingredients as in Step 3; microwave at 100% power 5 minutes, stirring after 3 minutes.

3. Assemble crepes as in Step 4; place in 2-quart shallow microwave-proof dish. Microwave at 100% power 4 minutes, or until filling is hot.

Empañada

1 tablespoon butter
2 tablespoons **LAWRY'S® Minced Onion with Green Onion Flakes**
¼ pound lean ground beef
1 package (10 oz.) frozen chopped spinach, drained thoroughly
1 teaspoon **LAWRY'S® Pinch of Herbs**
¼ teaspoon **LAWRY'S® Seasoned Salt**
⅛ teaspoon **LAWRY'S® Seasoned Pepper**
⅓ cup sour cream
1 egg, beaten
¼ cup grated Parmesan cheese
1 frozen deep dish pie shell, thawed

In a medium skillet, melt butter and sauté **Minced Onion with Green Onion Flakes** until butter is absorbed. Add ground beef, cook until brown and crumbly; drain fat. Add spinach, seasonings, sour cream, egg, and cheese; blend well. Remove pastry shell from foil pan and place flat on baking sheet. Spoon filling on half of the pastry, fold the other half over and press edges together to form a seal. Pierce several holes in top. Bake in a 350° F oven for 25 minutes or until golden brown. *Makes 2 generous servings*

Picadillo

1 pound lean ground beef
¼ teaspoon **LAWRY'S® Garlic Powder with Parsley**
¼ cup **LAWRY'S® Minced Onion with Green Onion Flakes**
1 package **LAWRY'S® Mexican Rice Seasoning Mix**
12 small pimiento-stuffed green olives, quartered
Pinch of leaf oregano, crushed
LAWRY'S® Seasoned Salt, to taste
LAWRY'S® Seasoned Pepper, to taste
1 cup red wine
1 cup raisins, plumped in water
1 small green bell pepper, chopped
Chopped watercress, for garnish

Brown ground beef, then add **Garlic Powder with Parsley**, **Minced Onion with Green Onion Flakes**, **Mexican Rice Seasoning Mix** and oregano; blend thoroughly. Add remaining ingredients except green pepper and watercress. Simmer mixture over medium heat 20 minutes, stirring occasionally.

Add green pepper during the last 5 minutes, cooking just until heated. Serve over rice and garnish with chopped watercress.
Makes 6 servings

Mexican Stuffed Peppers

2 medium green peppers
Boiling salted water
1 can (8 oz.) kidney beans
¼ pound ground beef
½ teaspoon chili powder
1 tablespoon oil
¾ teaspoon salt
¾ cup **MINUTE® Rice**
6 tablespoons grated Cheddar cheese
1 can (8 oz.) stewed tomatoes
½ teaspoon chili powder

Cut peppers in half lengthwise and remove stems and seeds. Cook in boiling salted water for 10 minutes, or until just tender. Drain and set aside.

Drain beans, reserving liquid. Add water to liquid to make ¾ cup. Brown beef lightly with ½ teaspoon chili powder in oil in small skillet; add salt and the measured liquid. Bring to a boil; stir in rice, cover and simmer 5 minutes. Stir in ¼ cup of the cheese and spoon meat mixture into peppers. Pour tomatoes, the kidney beans and ½ teaspoon chili powder into the skillet. Place stuffed peppers in the skillet; sprinkle with remaining cheese. Cover and simmer 5 minutes. *Makes 2 servings*

Pork

Mexicali Pizza

1 package (16⅞ oz.) **CHEF BOY-AR-DEE® Complete Sausage Pizza Mix**
1 cup cooked or canned corn
1 tablespoon minced green pepper
1 tablespoon minced pimiento

Preheat oven to 425°F. Prepare PIZZA FLOUR MIX as package directs. Mix together corn, green pepper, pimiento and pizza sauce. Spread mixture evenly over prepared crust. Sprinkle canned grated cheese from package over top. Bake for 16-20 minutes.
Serves four to six

Sausage Olé

1½ lb. **HILLSHIRE FARM® Hot Smoked Sausage**, chopped
½ cup chopped onion
2 cans (8 oz. each) tomato sauce
½ tsp. oregano
1 can (15 oz.) kidney beans, drained (optional)
1 pkg. (8 oz.) tortilla chips, crushed
2 cups (8 oz.) Cheddar or Monterey Jack cheese, shredded
Sour cream, shredded lettuce and sliced ripe olives (optional)

Place sausage in skillet with onion and lightly brown. Add tomato sauce, oregano and kidney beans. Simmer 5 minutes. Place ⅔ of the crushed tortilla chips in bottom of 2 qt. buttered baking dish. Layer ½ the cheese over chips. Pour sausage mixture over cheese. Layer on remaining chips and remaining cheese. Bake at 350° for 10-15 minutes or until heated through. Top with sour cream, shredded lettuce and sliced ripe olives, if desired.
Yield: 6 servings

MICROWAVE METHOD:
In a 2 quart casserole combine sausage and onion and microwave, uncovered, HIGH, 3 minutes; drain. Add tomato sauce, oregano and kidney beans. Microwave, covered, HIGH, 4-5 minutes or until bubbly, stirring once. Assemble as above but reserve top layer of cheese. Microwave, covered, HIGH, 5-7 minutes or until hot. Sprinkle with cheese and allow to stand, covered, 3-5 minutes before serving.

Empañada Grande *(front)*, Brandy Fiesta Salad *(back right)*, Sopaipillas with Brandy Anise Sauce *(center)*, Sweet Brandy Buns *(right)*, Brandied Mexican Chocolate *(left)*, Brandy Piñata Pralines *(front left)*, Brandy Cake de los Reyes *(back left)*
The Christian Brothers® *(Fromm and Sichel, Inc.)*

White Sangria *(left)*, ReaLime® Guacamole *(middle)*, Seviche *(right)*
ReaLime® *(Borden Inc.)*

Rio Grande Dip
(Michigan Bean Commission)

Nachos
Corn Chex® *(Ralston Purina Co.)*

Cheese Sticks Olé
Taco-Mate® *(Fisher Cheese Co.)*

Mexican Cucumber Sticks
Calavo®-Burnac *(Calavo Growers of California)*

Mexicana Layered Dip
Wolf® Brand *(Wolf Brand Products)*

Valencia Mushrooms
Hiram Walker *(Hiram Walker & Sons, Inc.)*

Guacamole Dip (or Salad) *(front left)*, Chili/Chili con Queso Dip *(back left)*, Bean Dip *(right)*
Gebhardt®'s *(Gebhardt Mexican Foods)*

Mexican-Style Taco Salad
Pepperidge Farm® *(Pepperidge Farm, Inc.)*

Gazpacho Garden Salad
ReaLemon® *(Borden Inc.)*

Hot Mexican Salad
Premium *(Nabisco Brands, Inc.)*

Spicy Hot Taco Salad
Betty Crocker® Hamburger Helper® *(General Mills, Inc.)*

Nopalitos Salad
La Preferida® *(La Preferida, Inc.)*

Black Bean Vegetable Soup
(Michigan Bean Commission)

Tortilla Soup
Old El Paso® *(Pet Incorporated)*

37

Flautas with Pork Filling *(right)*, Ortega Guacamole *(left)*
Ortega *(Heublein Inc.)*

Quesadillas
Jimmy Dean® *(Jimmy Dean Meat Company, Inc.)*

Mr. McIlhenny's Chili
Tabasco® *(McIlhenny Co.)*

Frijoles and Zucchini Bake
(Michigan Bean Commission)

Stokely's Finest® Mexican Corn Bread *(back)*, Texas Chili *(front)*
Stokely's Finest® *(Stokely-Van Camp, Inc.)*

One Dish Roni-Mac® Chili
American Beauty® Roni-Mac® *(The Pillsbury Company)*

La Preferida® Mexican Pizza
La Preferida® *(La Preferida, Inc.)*

Deep Dish Mexican Pizza
Wyler's® *(Borden Inc.)*

Tacos Alchili
Wolf® Brand *(Wolf Brand Products)*

Acapulco Salad *(top)*, Tortilla Pie *(bottom)*, Mexican Pudding *(middle right)*
Del Monte *(Del Monte Corporation)*

Picadillo
Lawry's® *(Lawry's Foods, Inc.)*

Acapulco Fillets
Booth® *(Booth Fisheries Corp.)*

Chicken Chilies Rellenos *(front)*, Tomato Chili Cheese Soup *(back)*
Old El Paso®, **Pet**® *(Pet Incorporated)*

''Chili Kahlúa®''
Kahlúa® *(Maidstone Wine & Spirits, Inc.)*

Mexicali Tacos
Campbell's *(Campbell Soup Co.)*

Huevos California
Ore-Ida® *(Ore-Ida Foods, Inc.)*

Tacos
Gerber *(Gerber Products Company)*

Crab Enchiladas
(Florida Department of Natural Resources)

42

Wiener Enchilada Casserole
Oscar Mayer *(Oscar Mayer Foods Corporation)*

Lipton® Rice Olé
Lipton® *(Thomas J. Lipton, Inc.)*

Sausages Español
Jones *(Jones Dairy Farm)*

Tamale Pollo Casserole
Wolf® Brand *(Wolf Brand Products)*

Mexican Fiesta Turkey Wings
Louis Rich™ *(Louis Rich Co., Div. of Oscar Mayer Foods Corp.)*

Mexican Pie
Betty Crocker® Potato Buds® *(General Mills, Inc.)*

Tostadas with Pork
(National Pork Producers Council)

Mexican-Style Duckling with Pineapple Orange Sauce
(National Duckling Council)

Mexican Sardine-Stuffed Tomato Cups
Port Clyde, Holmes (Port Clyde Foods, Inc.)

Huevos Rancheros
Lea & Perrins (Lea & Perrins, Inc.)

Rum Flan *(back left)*, Mexican Corn Bread *(middle)*, Veracruz Shrimp *(front left)*, Pimiento Cheese Dip *(front right)*
Pet®, Old El Paso®, Old El Paso Nachips® *(Pet Incorporated)*

Chili *(back)*, Chicken Mole *(front)*
Nestlé Choco-Bake *(The Nestlé Company)*

Rio Grande Stew
Wyler's® *(Borden Inc.)*

46

Mexican Stuffed Zucchini
Old El Paso® *(Pet Incorporated)*

Mexican Hot Pepper Bread
Kellogg's Corn Flakes®, **Kellogg's**® *(Kellogg Company)*

Crispy Taco Drumsticks
Perdue® *(Perdue Farms Inc.)*

Low-Sodium Chocolate Mousse
Angostura® *(Angostura International Ltd.)*

Margarita Pie
Wise®, **Eagle**® *(Borden Inc.)*

Kahlúa® Wafers/Kahlúa® Dip
Kahlúa® *(Maidstone Wine & Spirits, Inc.)*

Banana Rum Cake (Torta Al Ron)
Chiquita® *(Chiquita Brands, Inc.)*

Frosted Oranges Saronno
Amaretto Di Saronno® *(Foreign Vintages, Inc.)*

Rice with Milk Pudding (Arroz con Leche)
Knox® *(Thomas J. Lipton, Inc.)*

Chex®
Mexican Supper Pie

½ pound (8 oz.) mild pork sausage
⅓ cup chopped onion
3 eggs
¾ teaspoon ground cumin
1½ cups milk
1½ cups **CORN CHEX® Cereal**
2 tablespoons chopped green chilies
1 tablespoon chopped pimiento
1 (9-inch) unbaked pastry shell
1 cup (4 oz.) shredded Monterey Jack cheese
¼ cup thinly sliced pitted ripe olives

Preheat oven to 425°. In medium-size skillet crumble pork sausage; add onion. Cook and stir until onion is tender and meat is no longer pink. Drain drippings. Set aside.

In large bowl beat eggs and cumin. Stir in milk. Add **CHEX®**, chilies, pimiento and cooked sausage. Mix well. Pour into shell. Sprinkle with cheese. Top with olives. Bake 15 minutes. Reduce oven to 375°. Bake additional 30 to 35 minutes or until knife inserted in center comes out clean. Let cool 10 minutes before serving. *Makes 6 servings*

JONES
DAIRY FARM
Sausages Español

1 package (16 oz.) **JONES Dinner Sausages**
½ cup onion, coarsely chopped
½ cup celery, coarsely chopped
¾ cup green pepper, coarsely chopped
1 can (16 oz.) tomatoes, coarsely chopped, with juice
1 can (8 oz.) tomato sauce
2 cloves garlic, finely chopped
½ tsp. dried thyme
Salt, pepper, and a dash of hot pepper sauce to taste

Prepare **JONES Dinner Sausages** according to directions, remove from pan and keep warm. Pour off all but 2 tablespoons of fat, add onions, celery and green pepper, sauté for 5 minutes. Add tomatoes with juice, tomato sauce, garlic, thyme. Simmer, uncovered, for 15 minutes. Season to taste, return sausages to pan long enough to reheat. Serve with rice or pasta, accompanied by green salad.

Sausage con Queso

2 pounds **TENNESSEE PRIDE® Country Sausage**
1 pound processed cheese
¼ cup picante sauce
Milk to thin sauce

Roll **TENNESSEE PRIDE® Country Sausage** into ¾-inch balls. Brown until done, drain and set aside. Melt cheese over very low heat. Stir in picante sauce, adjusting amount to taste. Thin sauce with small amount of milk, if necessary. Add sausage balls, coating all sides. For a main dish, serve over rice.

Sausage Supper Olé

1 (7 ounce) pkg. *or* 2 cups uncooked elbow macaroni, cooked as package directs and drained
½ pound bulk pork sausage, cooked and crumbled
4 eggs, well beaten
2 cups shredded **COUNTY LINE® Sharp Cheddar Cheese**
¼ cup chopped green chilies
¼ tsp. pepper
1 (8 ounce) container sour cream, at room temperature
1 (2.8 ounce) can French fried onions

Preheat oven to 350°. Place cooked macaroni and sausage in 9-inch square baking dish. In medium bowl, combine eggs, **COUNTY LINE® Sharp Cheddar Cheese**, chilies and pepper; fold in sour cream. Pour evenly over macaroni and sausage. Bake uncovered 25 to 30 minutes or until hot. Top with onions; bake 5 minutes longer. Refrigerate leftovers. *Serves 6*

Mexican Melt

1 (6 inch diam.) corn tortilla (not fried)
1 slice (1 oz.) **KAHN'S® Cooked Ham**, cut into small pieces
1 oz. Cheddar cheese, grated
2 Tbsp. chopped green onion

Place tortilla in nonstick baking dish. Top with ham, cheese, and onion. Bake at 350° for 10-15 minutes or until cheese is melted. *Makes 1 serving*

Calories: 210 calories per serving

Easy Oven Barbecue Ribs

Brush ribs liberally with **FIGARO LIQUID BARBECUE SMOKE**. Relax, allow 30 minutes for flavor to penetrate. Salt and pepper. Fry salt pork in pan until brown, remove and place ribs in pan of hot grease and quickly fry brown. Pour ½ cup of water in pan and for each pound of ribs, add one teaspoon of **FIGARO LIQUID BARBECUE SMOKE**. Place lid on pan and cook in oven about 350°. Baste often while cooking. Uncover pan about 30 minutes before done.

Mexicali Pork Bake

6 loin pork chops
3 garlic cloves, crushed
½ cup **HOLLAND HOUSE®** White Cooking Wine
1½ tablespoons chili powder
1 teaspoon oregano
1 6-ounce can tomato puree
1 8-ounce can tomato sauce
2 tablespoons lemon juice
Mexicali stuffing*

Place pork chops in a greased 9 x 12 x 3-inch baking dish. Mix remaining ingredients together, pour over chops, cover and refrigerate 2 to 3 hours. Turn several times. To bake, place each chop, fat edge up, at one end of the baking pan and spoon stuffing between standing chops. Bake, uncovered, in 350° oven for 1 hour, or until done, basting every 15 minutes with pan juices.

Serves 3 to 4

*Mexicali Stuffing

2 cups soft bread crumbs
¼ cup chopped celery
¼ cup chopped green chillies
2 tablespoons chopped parsley
Salt and pepper to taste
⅛ teaspoon cayenne pepper
1 tablespoon sugar
¼ cup **HOLLAND HOUSE®** White Cooking Wine

Combine stuffing ingredients in a large mixing bowl and toss lightly with fork until moist. Spoon between chops to bake.

Spanish Style Pork Chops

4 rib pork chops, cut ¾ to 1-inch thick
1 tablespoon cooking oil
1 medium onion, sliced thin
Salt
Pepper
1 can (15½ ounces) **AUNT NELLIE'S®** Sloppy Joe Sandwich Sauce
⅓ cup beef bouillon
2 tablespoons flour
½ cup sliced pimiento stuffed olives

Trim excess fat from meat. In large skillet, brown chops well in hot oil. Remove chops. In same skillet, cook onion until crisp-tender; drain off fat. Return chops to skillet. Season with salt and pepper. Cover with onions. Combine Sandwich Sauce, bouillon and flour; pour over chops. Add olives. Cover. Simmer 1½ hours or until meat is tender.   *4 servings*

Chili

Mr. McIlhenny's Chili

3 pounds lean stewing beef, well-trimmed, cut in 1-inch cubes
¼ cup salad oil
1 cup chopped onion
3 cloves garlic, minced
4 to 6 tablespoons chili powder
2 teaspoons salt
2 teaspoons ground cumin
2 teaspoons **TABASCO®** Pepper Sauce
1 can (4 ounces) green chilies, seeded and chopped
1 quart water

Garnish:
¼ cup chopped onion

In large saucepan, brown beef in oil. Add remaining ingredients and mix well. Bring to a boil, reduce heat and simmer uncovered 1½ to 2 hours until meat is tender. Garnish with chopped onion and serve with a bottle of **TABASCO®** sauce on the side.

Yield: 4 to 6 servings

Sausage Chili

2 lb. **BOB EVANS FARMS®** Roll Sausage (Original Recipe or Zesty Hot)
1 lb., 14 oz. can red kidney beans
1½ cups tomato puree
12 oz. can tomato paste
2 tsp. chili powder
1 tsp. salt
2 Tbsp. sugar
2 medium onions, diced
3 cups water

Crumble **BOB EVANS FARMS®** Sausage in a skillet, cook until tender and lightly browned. Add remaining ingredients to a large pot and bring to a full boil. To enhance the flavor, let cook. Refrigerate overnight, reheat the next day. This chili will keep refrigerated for several days or it may be frozen.

Yield: 14 8-oz. serving

Chili

2 measuring tablespoons vegetable oil
1 medium onion, chopped
2 garlic cloves, minced
1 pound ground beef
1 16-ounce can kidney beans, drained
1 16-ounce can tomato puree
1 6-ounce can tomato paste
1 4-ounce can chopped green chili peppers, seeded and drained
½ cup water
2 envelopes (2 ounces) **NESTLÉ CHOCO-BAKE**, divided
2 measuring tablespoons chili powder
1 measuring tablespoon beef-flavored instant bouillon

Heat oil in a large skillet; add onion and garlic and sauté until tender. Add ground beef; cook over medium heat until meat is evenly browned. Drain off excess fat. Stir in beans, tomato puree, tomato paste, chili peppers, water, 1 envelope **NESTLÉ CHOCO-BAKE**, chili powder and bouillon; mix well. Simmer uncovered 30 minutes, stirring occasionally. Stir in remaining **NESTLÉ CHOCO-BAKE** and heat through. Serve with corn chips or over hot rice. *Makes 4 to 6 servings*

Mazola.

Vegetarian Chili

⅓ cup **MAZOLA® Corn Oil**
2 cups coarsely chopped onion
2 medium green peppers, cut into 1-inch strips (2 cups)
3 cloves garlic, minced or pressed
3 cups coarsely shredded carrots
1 large zucchini, diced (2 cups)
1 cup sliced celery
3 cans (1 lb. each) tomatoes, undrained, coarsely chopped
2 cans (4 oz. each) hot green chilies, drained, minced
1½ teaspoons salt
1 teaspoon crushed dried red pepper
1 teaspoon dried oregano leaves
2 cans (1 lb. each) white and/or red kidney beans, drained
1 can (1 lb.) pinto beans, drained

In 8-quart saucepot heat corn oil over medium heat. Add onion, green peppers and garlic. Stirring occasionally, cook 5 minutes or until tender. Stir in carrots, zucchini, celery, tomatoes, chilies, salt, red pepper and oregano. Stirring occasionally, cook over medium heat 30 minutes. Add beans; cook 30 minutes longer. If desired, serve over rice. *Makes about 12 (1-cup) servings*

Note: Chili may be frozen in tightly covered containers. Thaw completely before heating.

"Chili Kahlúa®"

¼ cup vegetable oil
2 onions, chopped
2 cloves garlic, minced
2 pounds ground beef
½ bell pepper, chunked
1 1-pound-12-ounce can tomatoes, partially drained
1 tablespoon tomato paste
¼ cup parsley, chopped
1 teaspoon marjoram, crushed
1 teaspoon oregano, crushed
1 teaspoon cumin, crushed
3 tablespoons chili powder
2 teaspoons salt
1 scant teaspoon red cayenne pepper
½ cup **KAHLÚA®**
1 1-pound-11-ounce can red kidney beans, partially drained
Garnish: grated Cheddar cheese, chopped onion

In a 4-quart pot, heat oil, add onions and garlic and sauté until soft. Add meat, crumbling to separate particles and brown. Add bell peppers, tomatoes, tomato paste, parsley, marjoram, oregano, cumin, chili powder, salt and cayenne pepper, then mix thoroughly. Add **KAHLÚA®** and increase heat so that mixture simmers. Add beans and simmer, partially covered, for 45 minutes.

Serve in bowls garnished with grated cheese and chopped onions. Or fill corn or flour tortillas and roll into enchiladas. Place in a baking dish, seam-side down and cover with your favorite enchilada sauce flavored with 2 tablespoons **KAHLÚA®**. Top with Cheddar cheese and place under broiler for 3 minutes or until cheese has melted. *Yields 2½ quarts or 6 servings*

Budweiser.
Chili with Beer

2 pounds dried kidney beans
2 tablespoons salt
2 pounds ground beef
4 medium onions (about 1 pound) chopped
¼ cup sugar
3 garlic cloves, minced
3 tablespoons chili powder
1 tablespoon dry mustard
2 cans or bottles (12 ounces each) **BUDWEISER® Beer**
2 cans (6 ounces each) tomato paste
2 medium green peppers, chopped

Soak beans overnight in water to cover, adding more water as needed to keep beans immersed. In same water, simmer beans with 1 tablespoon salt, for 1 hour, or until tender. Add more water as needed to keep beans covered. Meanwhile, brown beef and onion in a skillet, using a little oil if meat is very lean. Pour off fat. Add sugar, garlic, chili powder, dry mustard and 1 tablespoon salt; stir. Add 1 can **BUDWEISER® Beer**. Cover and simmer 30 minutes. Stir tomato paste into beans. Add green pepper and meat mixture. Cover and simmer 30 minutes (leave uncovered if too "soupy"), adding remaining 1 can **BUDWEISER® Beer** during last 5 minutes. Adjust seasonings, if desired. *About five quarts*

Texas Chili

½ pound lean ground beef
½ cup chopped onion
½ cup chopped green pepper
¼ cup chopped celery
1 package (1¼ ounces) chili seasoning mix
1 can (8 ounces) **STOKELY'S FINEST® Tomato Sauce**
1 can (15 ounces) **STOKELY'S FINEST® Dark Red Kidney Beans**
For garnish: chopped onion, chopped green pepper, grated cheese, or commercial sour cream

Place beef, onion, green pepper, and celery in large skillet. Cook over medium heat, stirring constantly, until meat is browned and vegetables are tender. Drain excess fat. Stir in remaining ingredients, cover, and simmer 30 minutes. Top with chopped onion, chopped green pepper, grated cheese, or sour cream. *4 servings*

MICROWAVE METHOD:
Crumble beef in 1½-quart casserole. Add onion, green pepper, and celery. Microcook, covered, 6 minutes, stirring twice. Drain excess fat. Stir in remaining ingredients, cover, and microcook 5 minutes, stirring once. Top with chopped onion, chopped green pepper, grated cheese, or sour cream.

Turkey Chili

2 cups diced, roasted **BUTTERBALL® SWIFT'S PREMIUM® Turkey**
1 cup chopped onion
½ cup chopped celery
1 clove garlic, minced
2 tablespoons butter or margarine
10¾ ounce can condensed cream of tomato soup
8 ounce can tomato sauce
1 tablespoon chili powder
¼ teaspoon salt
2 cans (16 ounces each) kidney beans

Panfry onion, celery and garlic in butter until lightly browned. Stir in soup and sauce, turkey, chili powder and salt. For a future meal, pour half the mixture into a 1 pint freezer container. Cool, label and freeze.

To serve: Add one 16 ounce can kidney beans with liquid to remaining mixture. Cook, uncovered, over low heat, simmering gently for 30 minutes.   *Makes 3 to 4 servings*

To serve frozen Chili: Thaw chili, add remaining can of kidney beans and follow same procedure as above.

Makes 3 to 4 servings

Open Pit® Chili con Carne

½ pound ground beef
¼ cup chopped onion
2 tablespoons chopped green pepper
1 can (8¾ oz.) red kidney beans
1 can (8¼ oz.) whole tomatoes
½ cup **OPEN PIT® Barbecue Sauce**, any flavor
1 teaspoon chili powder
¼ teaspoon salt

Brown beef, onion and green pepper in skillet or heavy saucepan. Pour off any excess fat. Stir in remaining ingredients. Cover and simmer 30 minutes, stirring occasionally. Serve with grilled sausages, if desired.   *Makes 2¾ cups*

One Dish Roni-Mac® Chili

1 lb. ground beef
½ cup chopped onion
28-oz. can tomatoes, undrained
15-oz. can kidney beans, undrained and cut up
1 cup water
6-oz. can tomato paste
1½ cups **AMERICAN BEAUTY® RONI-MAC®**
1 tablespoon chili powder
1 teaspoon salt
½ teaspoon oregano

In Dutch oven, brown ground beef with onion; drain. Add remaining ingredients. Stirring frequently, bring to a boil over high heat. Cover and cook over low heat, stirring occasionally, for 25 to 30 minutes or until **RONI-MAC®** is tender.   *8 servings*

HIGH ALTITUDE—Above 3500 Feet: no change.

NUTRITIONAL INFORMATION PER SERVING			
SERVING SIZE:		PERCENT U.S. RDA	
⅛ OF RECIPE		PER SERVING	
Calories	273	Protein	26
Protein	17 g	Vitamin A	32
Carbohydrate	31 g	Vitamin C	47
Fat	9 g	Thiamine	16
Sodium	430 mg	Riboflavin	12
Potassium	707 mg	Niacin	23
		Calcium	4
		Iron	22

Chilly Day Chili

2 medium onions, chopped
1 green pepper, coarsely diced
1 tablespoon salad oil
2 pounds lean ground beef
1 can (1 pound) tomatoes
1 can (15 ounces) tomato sauce
½ cup **HEINZ Tomato Ketchup**
1 tablespoon chili powder
2 teaspoons salt
¼ teaspoon pepper
2 cans (15½ ounces each) kidney beans, partially drained

In large kettle or Dutch oven, sauté onions and green pepper in oil until tender. Add beef stirring lightly to break up. Cover; simmer about 30 minutes or until meat loses color. Drain excess fat. Add tomatoes and next 5 ingredients. Simmer, uncovered, 30 minutes, stirring occasionally. Add kidney beans; simmer an additional 15 minutes.   *Makes 10-12 servings (about 2½ quarts)*

Note: Recipe is a mild flavored chili. Additional chili powder may be added for a spicier dish.

Poultry

Coronado Casserole

1 can (15 ounces) tomato sauce
½ cup chicken broth
1 cup chopped onions
1 can (4 ounces) diced green chiles
2 teaspoons salt
½ teaspoon *each* ground cumin and oregano
2 cups boned cooked chicken
3 cups cooked **DORE® Rice**
1 cup sour cream
2 cups grated Cheddar cheese, divided
1½ cups crushed corn chips

CONVENTIONAL METHOD:

Combine tomato sauce, broth, onions, green chiles, and seasonings. Cook over low heat about 10 minutes. Add chicken. Set aside. Mix rice and sour cream. Spoon into a shallow 2-quart casserole. Sprinkle with 1 cup cheese; pour sauce over all. Top with remaining cheese. Sprinkle with corn chips. Bake at 350° for 25 minutes.

MICROWAVE METHOD:

Combine tomato sauce, broth, onions, green chiles, and seasonings in a 1-quart microproof casserole. Cook on HIGH (maximum power) for 10 minutes or until mixture boils. Stir in chicken. Set aside. Mix rice and sour cream in a shallow 2-quart microproof casserole. Sprinkle with 1 cup cheese; pour sauce over all. Top with remaining cheese; sprinkle with corn chips. Cook on HIGH for 5 minutes. *Makes 6 to 8 servings*

Roast Chicken, Spanish Style

1 4½ to 5-pound roasting chicken
Salt and pepper
1 clove garlic
4 tablespoons **FILIPPO BERIO Olive Oil**
½ teaspoon oregano
1 medium onion, sliced
1 cup Italian tomatoes, cut small
2 medium-sized green peppers, cut up
¾ pound small mushrooms (washed and drained)

Dress and clean chicken. Season inside and out with salt and pepper. Rub outside with a cut clove of garlic. Roll in olive oil to which oregano has been added.

Roast in open pan in hot oven (450°F.). When browned, reduce heat to 375°F., add onion and tomatoes. Cover and continue roasting 1 to 1¼ hours, or till tender.

Twenty minutes before chicken is finished, add the green peppers and mushrooms. *Serves 6*

Spanish Chicken*

3 tablespoons salad or olive oil
2 (2½ to 3 lb. each) chickens, cut into serving-size pieces
1 cup chopped onion
1 clove garlic, crushed
1 can (1 lb. 12 oz.) tomatoes, broken up
1 can (10½ oz.) condensed chicken broth
½ cup water
3 tablespoons **LEA & PERRINS Worcestershire Sauce**
2 tablespoons chopped parsley
1 teaspoon salt
½ teaspoon oregano leaves, crumbled
2 cups raw, regular, cooking rice
1 package (10 oz.) frozen peas, thawed
1 package (9 oz.) frozen artichoke hearts, thawed

In a large skillet heat oil. Add chicken and brown well on all sides. Remove chicken to a 3-quart casserole; set aside. To the skillet add onion and garlic; sauté 5 minutes. Stir in tomatoes, broth, water, **LEA & PERRINS**, parsley, salt and oregano. Heat, stirring occasionally, until mixture comes to a boil. Pour over chicken. Stir in rice. Cover tightly and bake in a preheated moderate oven (350°F.) 30 minutes. Remove cover, fluff rice with fork. Stir in peas and artichokes. Replace cover and bake 10 minutes longer. *Yield: 6 to 8 portions*

*May be prepared in advance of serving

PERDUE

Chicken Wings Mexicana

12 **PERDUE® Chicken Wings**
2 tablespoons oil
1 medium onion, chopped
½ cup chopped green pepper
1 medium clove garlic, minced
1 can (16 ounces) whole tomatoes
1½ cups water
1 cup raw long grain rice
1 teaspoon salt
½ teaspoon chili powder
1 package (10 ounces) frozen peas, partially thawed

Wash chicken; pat dry. In Dutch oven, brown chicken in oil and cook onion, green pepper and garlic until onion is tender. Add tomatoes, water, rice, salt and chili powder. Bring to boil. Reduce heat, cover and simmer 30 minutes or until chicken and rice are tender. Add peas. Cook 5 minutes longer. *Serves 4*

Arroz con Pollo

2½ pounds cut-up chicken
1 envelope **SHAKE 'N BAKE® Seasoned Coating Mix for Chicken—Barbecue Style**
2 tablespoons butter or margarine
1½ cups **MINUTE® Rice**
½ cup chopped onion
1 small clove garlic, crushed (optional)
1½ cups water
1 package (10 oz.) **BIRDS EYE® 5 Minute Sweet Green Peas**, thawed
1 can (4 oz.) sliced mushrooms, drained
2 chicken bouillon cubes
Pinch of ground bay leaves (optional)

Coat chicken with seasoned coating mix as directed on package. Place in 13 × 9-inch pan. Sprinkle evenly with any remaining mix. Bake at 350° for 50 minutes, or until chicken is tender. Meanwhile, melt butter in skillet or saucepan. Add rice, onion and garlic and sauté until rice is lightly browned. Add remaining ingredients. Bring to a boil. Remove from heat; cover and let stand 5 minutes. Serve with the chicken.

Makes 5 cups rice mixture plus chicken or 4 servings

COOKIN' GOOD™
GRADE A CHICKEN

Chicken and Yellow Rice
(Arroz con Pollo)

2½-3 pounds of your favorite **COOKIN' GOOD**™
  Parts
1 teaspoon salt
Juice of 1 lime
2 medium onions, chopped
1 medium green pepper, chopped
2 cloves garlic, pressed
½ cup tomato sauce or 1 ripe tomato chopped
¼ cup of olive or vegetable oil
3 cups chicken broth
1 can (8 oz.) sweet peas
1 can (4 oz.) pimientos
2 tablespoons parsley, chopped
1 pound rice
½ teaspoon saffron
2 teaspoons salt
¼ teaspoon black pepper

Cut chicken in small serving pieces. Sprinkle with 1 teaspoon of salt and lime juice. Set aside for 1 hour. Heat oil in a large heavy skillet over medium heat. Add garlic, chopped onions and green pepper. Cook over medium heat until onion is tender, but not browned. Add tomato sauce or chopped tomato and parsley. Cook 5 minutes, stirring often. Add chicken broth, half of the sweet peas with its liquid, saffron, pepper, and salt. Bring to a boil. Add rice. Cover and simmer about 20 minutes or until rice is tender and liquid is absorbed. If extra liquid is needed add additional broth. Serve garnished with peas and pimientos. *Serves 4*

Souverain® Paella

1 (3 pound) broiler-fryer chicken, cut up
⅓ cup **PLANTERS® Peanut Oil**
¾ cup chopped onion
1 clove garlic, minced
2 cups long grain rice
4 cups water
4 chicken bouillon cubes
2 teaspoons salt
½ teaspoon paprika
¼ teaspoon ground saffron
2 pounds fresh shrimp with tails, shelled and deveined
1 package (10 oz.) frozen artichoke hearts, defrosted
2 cups fresh cut green beans
2 medium tomatoes, peeled and chopped
1 cup **SOUVERAIN® Chardonnay**
12 small clams, scrubbed

Debone chicken breast and cut into 5 pieces. In a large skillet heat **PLANTERS® Peanut Oil** over medium high heat. Add chicken pieces and sauté until golden brown. Remove chicken from skillet. Add onion and garlic to skillet and cook until tender. Stir in rice until grains are well coated. Remove skillet from heat.

In a Dutch oven bring water to a boil. Mix in bouillon cubes,

salt, paprika and saffron. Stir in chicken, rice mixture, shrimp, artichoke hearts, green beans and tomatoes. Simmer over medium high heat for 15 minutes. Cover and chill until ready to use.

Stir **SOUVERAIN® Chardonnay** into mixture in Dutch oven; place clams on top. Cover and simmer 20 to 25 minutes, or until most of the liquid is absorbed. Serve immediately.

Makes 8 servings

Chicken Tamale Casserole

2 tablespoons corn oil margarine
2 onions, finely chopped
2 buds garlic, minced
1 green bell pepper, seeded and chopped
1 28-ounce can whole tomatoes, drained and chopped
  (2½ cups)
1 cup fresh or fresh-frozen corn kernels
¼ teaspoon freshly ground black pepper
1 teaspoon salt
2 tablespoons chili powder
1 teaspoon ground cumin
½ cup yellow corn meal
1 cup chicken stock
3 cups coarsely chopped cooked chicken or turkey
  without skin
1½ cups non-fat milk
1 tablespoon corn oil margarine
1 tablespoon **SWEETLITE**™ **Liquid Fructose**
1 teaspoon salt
½ cup yellow corn meal
1 cup grated sharp Cheddar cheese
2 eggs, lightly beaten

1. Preheat the oven to 375°. Heat the margarine in a large skillet.
2. Add the onion, garlic and green pepper and cook until the onions are a golden brown.
3. Add the tomatoes and corn kernels to the skillet.
4. Combine the pepper, salt, chili powder, cumin and corn meal and mix well.
5. Add the chicken stock to the corn meal mixture and pour into the skillet with the vegetables. Simmer, covered, for 10 minutes.
6. Add the chopped chicken or turkey and spoon into a 3-quart casserole.
7. In a saucepan, combine the milk, corn oil margarine, liquid fructose, salt and corn meal and cook slowly, stirring until thickened.
8. Remove from the heat, add the cheese and beaten eggs, mix well and pour over the chicken mixture in the casserole.
9. Bake, uncovered, for 30-40 minutes in the 375° oven or until golden brown on the top. *Makes 8 servings*

Note: If you are planning to make it in advance, the baking time will be longer when the ingredients are cold. Bake at 375° for 1 hour and 10 minutes or until bubbling hot.

Each serving contains approximately:
  1 fat exchange
  1 vegetable exchange
  1 bread exchange
  ½ high-fat meat exchange
  ¼ medium-fat meat exchange
  1½ low-fat meat exchanges
  290 calories
  116.25 mg. cholesterol

Tamale Pollo Casserole

1 cup finely crushed corn chips
1 15 oz. can WOLF® Brand Tamales
1 10 oz. can WOLF® Brand Plain Chili
1½ cups chopped cooked chicken
1 8 oz. can whole kernel corn, undrained
1 4 oz. can chopped green chilies, drained
1 cup (4 oz.) shredded Cheddar cheese

Sprinkle corn chips evenly onto bottom of 8-inch square baking dish. Unwrap tamales; arrange over corn chips. Combine remaining ingredients except cheese; mix well. Spoon over tamales. Bake in preheated moderate oven (350°F.) 20 minutes. Sprinkle with cheese; continue baking about 5 minutes. Serve with sour cream.

Serves 5 to 6

Crispy Taco Drumsticks

12 PERDUE® Chicken Drumsticks
½ cup milk
1 egg, beaten
½ teaspoon garlic salt
1 bag (7 ounces) taco flavored corn chips, finely crushed
¼ cup grated Parmesan cheese
½ cup oil

Wash chicken; pat dry. In shallow bowl or pie plate, combine milk, egg and salt. In another bowl, combine corn chips and cheese. Dip chicken into milk mixture, then coat with chip mixture. Heat oil in large skillet. Fry chicken in oil, turning once, until golden and tender, about 30 minutes. Drain on towels and serve. If desired, serve with heated canned taco sauce.   *Serves 4-6*

Nestlé
Chicken Mole

Chicken:
⅓ cup unsifted flour
3 measuring tablespoons chili powder, divided
2 measuring teaspoons salt
½ measuring teaspoon pepper
2 broiler-fryers (2½ to 3 pounds each), cut up
3 measuring tablespoons vegetable oil
1 cup chopped onion
3 garlic cloves, minced
¼ cup water

Chocolate Mole Sauce:
1 10-ounce can tomatoes and green chilies
1 cup tomato puree
1 6-ounce package (1 cup) NESTLÉ Semi-Sweet Real Chocolate Morsels
1 measuring teaspoon chicken-flavored instant bouillon (or 1 cube, crushed)

Garnish:
1 cup chopped peanuts

CHICKEN:
In a large bowl or plastic bag, combine flour, 1 measuring tablespoon chili powder, the salt and pepper. Add chicken pieces (2 to 3 at a time); coat well. Heat oil in a large skillet; brown half the chicken pieces on all sides over medium heat. Drain thoroughly on paper towels. Repeat with remaining chicken. In same skillet, sauté onion and garlic until golden. Return chicken to skillet. Add the water; simmer, covered, over medium heat about 35 to 40 minutes or until chicken is tender. Transfer to a serving platter and top with Chocolate Mole Sauce (below). Garnish each serving with chopped peanuts.

CHOCOLATE MOLE SAUCE:
In a small saucepan, combine tomatoes and green chilies, tomato puree, NESTLÉ Semi-Sweet Real Chocolate Morsels, remaining chili powder and bouillon. Cook over low heat until morsels melt and sauce is heated through.

Makes 6 to 8 servings and 3⅓ cups sauce

Note: This mole is milder in flavor than a traditional Mexican mole.

Best Foods®/HELLMANN'S®
El Paso Chicken Legs

4 cups corn chips, crushed
1½ teaspoons chili powder
½ teaspoon onion powder
¼ teaspoon garlic powder
6 broiler-fryer chicken legs
¼ cup BEST FOODS®/HELLMANN'S® Real Mayonnaise

In shallow dish or on sheet of waxed paper combine first 4 ingredients. Rinse chicken and pat dry. Brush all sides with Real Mayonnaise; coat with chip mixture. Place skin-side-up in shallow roasting pan. Bake in 425°F oven 45 minutes or until fork-tender.   *Makes 6 servings*

MICROWAVE METHOD:
Place 3 legs in oblong glass baking dish with thickest parts toward outside of dish. Microwave with full power 20 minutes, rotating dish after 10 minutes. Let stand 5 minutes. Repeat.

✳Yoplait®
Viva Chicken Tortilla

2 tablespoons chicken broth or water
2 cartons (6 ounces each) YOPLAIT® Plain Yogurt (about 1⅓ cups)
1 can (10¾ ounces) condensed cream of mushroom soup
1 can (10¾ ounces) condensed cream of chicken soup
1 jar (8 ounces) green salsa
1 medium onion, finely chopped
12 corn tortillas, cut into 1-inch strips
4 cups cut-up cooked chicken
4 cups shredded Cheddar cheese (16 ounces)
Spanish stuffed olives, sliced

Heat oven to 350°. Butter rectangular baking dish, 13x9x2 inches; spoon broth into dish. Mix yogurt, soups, salsa and onion. Layer ⅓ of the tortilla strips, 1⅓ cups of the chicken, about 1⅓ cups of the soup mixture and 1⅓ cups of the cheese in dish; repeat 2 times. Bake uncovered 40 minutes. Let stand 10 to 15 minutes before serving. Garnish with olives.   *8 servings*

Brandied Chicken Casserole

2½ to 3 pounds frying chicken pieces
¼ cup flour
1½ teaspoons seasoned salt
1 egg
2 tablespoons water
1 cup finely crushed corn chips
¼ cup shortening (half butter)
1 teaspoon onion powder
½ teaspoon chili powder
¼ teaspoon oregano
2 teaspoons cornstarch
⅓ cup California brandy
1 chicken bouillon cube, crumbled
1 (16 oz.) can tomato wedges
½ cup Jack or Muenster cheeses, pieces *or* grated

Dip chicken pieces in flour mixed with salt, then in egg beaten with water, and finally in corn chip crumbs to coat evenly. Let stand while measuring remaining ingredients. Brown coated chicken in shortening over moderate heat until golden brown. Turn only once; use broad spatula and turn gently to keep coating in place. Carefully arrange in shallow casserole, 10-inches diameter. Bake in hot oven (400 degrees F.), ½ hour. Combine seasonings with cornstarch and brandy. Add bouillon cube and tomatoes. Bring to boil and spoon over chicken. Continue baking until chicken is tender, 10 to 15 minutes longer. Dot with cheese and heat until melted *or* place under broiler a minute.

Makes 4 or 5 servings

Favorite recipe from **California Brandy Advisory Board**

South of the Border Chicken

⅓ cup **LAND O LAKES® Sweet Cream Butter**
1 cup crushed corn chips
1 tsp. *each* dried green onion and chili powder
¼ tsp. hot pepper sauce
3 to 3½ lb. frying chicken, cut into 8 pieces
¼ cup **LAND O LAKES® Sweet Cream Butter**
1 Tbsp. cornstarch
16-oz. can stewed tomatoes, undrained
4-oz. can chopped green chiles, undrained
½ cup pitted, sliced (¼ inch) ripe olives
¼ cup water
1 tsp. *each* garlic salt and chili powder

Preheat Oven: 350°. In ungreased 13x9 inch (3 qt.) baking dish melt ⅓ cup butter in preheated oven (5 to 7 min.). Meanwhile, in 9 inch pie pan combine crushed corn chips, green onion and 1 tsp. chili powder; stir to blend. Add hot pepper sauce to melted butter; stir to blend. Dip chicken pieces into melted butter, then roll into seasoned crumbs to coat. Place chicken, skin side up, in same baking dish; sprinkle with remaining crumb mixture. Bake near center of 350° oven for 65 to 80 min. or until chicken is fork tender. Meanwhile, in heavy 2-qt. saucepan melt ¼ cup butter over med. heat (4 to 5 min.). Add cornstarch; stir to blend. Add

remaining ingredients; stir to blend. Cook over med. heat, stirring occasionally, until mixture comes to a full boil (7 to 10 min.). Boil 1 min. To serve, pour hot sauce over chicken.

Yield: 4 to 6 servings

Nacho Chicken Bundles

4 whole chicken breasts halved, skinned and boned
1 (4 oz.) can whole green chilies
¼ lb. Monterey Jack cheese
1 7 oz. package of Nacho flavored tortilla chips, crushed fine
½ cup soybean oil margarine, melted

Flatten the chicken breasts between 2 pieces of plastic wrap until each chicken breast is ¼ inch thick. Cut the green chilies in half lengthwise and remove the seeds, cut into eight equal sized pieces. Cut the cheese into sticks about 1½ inches long and ½ inch wide. Place a piece of green chili and a stick of cheese on each of the flattened chicken pieces. Roll up to enclose filling and secure with wooden picks. Dip chicken bundles in melted soybean oil margarine, then roll in crushed tortilla chips. Place seam side down in a 9 × 5 inch baking dish. Drizzle remaining soybean oil margarine over chicken bundles and refrigerate from 2 to 12 hours. Bake in preheated oven at 400° for 20 minutes. *Makes 4 servings*

Favorite recipe from the **American Soybean Association**

Mexican Chicken in Crust

Tortilla Crust*
3 to 4 cups cut-up cooked chicken or turkey
1 cup dairy sour cream
½ cup finely chopped onion
1 can (10¾ ounces) condensed cream of chicken soup
1 can (4 ounces) whole green chilies, drained, seeded and chopped
2 cups shredded Monterey Jack cheese (8 ounces)
2 green onions (with tops), sliced (about ¼ cup)

Prepare Tortilla Crust: roll into rectangle, 20 x 13 inches. Fold rectangle crosswise into thirds. Place in ungreased rectangular baking dish, 11 x 7 x 1½ inches; unfold. Spread chicken over dough in dish.

Heat oven to 400°. Mix sour cream, onion, soup and chilies in 2-quart saucepan. Heat over medium heat, stirring occasionally, until hot; pour over chicken. Sprinkle with cheese and green onions. Fold ends of dough over filling to center of dish. Pinch ends of dough together at 7-inch sides of dish to seal. Cut slits in top to let steam escape. Bake until crust is golden brown, 45 to 50 minutes. *8 servings*

*Tortilla Crust

2 cups **GOLD MEDAL® All-Purpose Flour****
1 teaspoon salt
¾ teaspoon baking powder
⅓ cup shortening
½ to ¾ cup warm water

Mix flour, salt and baking powder; cut in shortening until mixture resembles fine crum's. Stir in water with fork until dough leaves side of bowl and rounds up into a ball. Turn dough onto lightly floured surface. Knead until smooth, 10 to 12 times. Cover and let rest about 15 minutes.

**If using self-rising flour, omit salt and baking powder.

Note: Unbleached flour can be used in this recipe.

HIGH ALTITUDE DIRECTIONS (3500 to 6500 feet): For all-purpose and unbleached flours, no adjustments are necessary. For self-rising flour, after rest period, knead dough 10 to 12 times. Continue as directed.

Chicken Chilies Rellenos

3 boneless chicken breasts, halved
1 can (7 oz.) **OLD EL PASO® Whole Green Chilies**
8 ounces Monterey Jack cheese or Cheddar cheese (cut into 6 strips, 3 x ½ x ½-inch)
2 cups all-purpose flour
2 teaspoons salt
1 teaspoon pepper
½ teaspoon paprika
2 eggs
½ cup milk
OLD EL PASO® Taco Sauce

Flatten chicken breasts with meat mallet. Slit chilies, removing seeds and ribs. Place a chili on each chicken breast. Place a piece of cheese on one end of a chili and roll the chicken breast jelly roll fashion. Secure with toothpicks. Season flour with salt, pepper and paprika. Beat together eggs and milk. Dip each chicken roll in egg then flour. Repeat. Deep fry at 400°F for 10 minutes until golden brown. Drain on paper towels. Serve with taco sauce.

Makes 6 chicken chilies rellenos

Whoppers®

Fiesta Chicken Casserole

1 3-4 lb. chicken, cut in serving pieces
1 7-oz. package of **WHOPPERS® Malted Milk Candy**, crushed
½ cup flour
1 egg beaten with 2 tablespoons of water
½ cup peanut or salad oil
1 medium onion, sliced

Sauce:

1 10-oz. can of tomatoes with green chiles or 1 8-oz. can of tomatoes and ¼ cup chopped green chiles
1 cup chicken broth
1 teaspoon chili powder
½ teaspoon ground cumin
2 teaspoons salt
½ teaspoon white pepper
1 oz. unsweetened chocolate, melted

Shake chicken in a paper bag with flour. Dip in beaten egg and roll in crushed **WHOPPERS®**. Brown *very quickly* in hot oil. Remember you are browning, not cooking. Place chicken in a 9 x 13 baking dish, or pottery for baking.

Sauté the onion rings until soft in remaining oil, drain and place on top of the chicken. Combine the remaining ingredients, including the leftover **WHOPPER®** crumbs, and 2 tablespoons of flour in a saucepan. Whisk until smooth and pour over chicken. Cover and bake for 1 hour at 375 degrees. *Serves 6*

Chicken Olé

3-4 lb. **TYSON® Country Fresh Chicken** (cut up)
½ cup melted butter
2-3 dashes hot sauce
1½ cups taco chips (crushed)
1½ tsp. chili powder
1 Tbsp. chives
Dash cayenne pepper
¼ cup onion flakes

Sauce:

½ stick (¼ cup) butter
1 Tbsp. cornstarch
1 16-oz. can stewed tomatoes
1 4-oz. can chopped green chilies
½ cup finely chopped green pepper
¾ cup sliced black olives
1 tsp. chili powder
1 tsp. garlic salt

Place chicken pieces in large casserole or baking dish. Add hot sauce to melted butter and pour over chicken, turning pieces to coat. In large bowl, combine crushed taco chips, chili powder, chives, pepper and onion flakes. Roll chicken pieces in crumb mixture to coat. Return to baking dish. Spread remaining coating over top. Bake at 350° for 1-1½ hours or until tender.

SAUCE:
For sauce, blend ¼ cup butter and cornstarch in heavy saucepan over medium heat. Add stewed tomatoes (with juice), green chilies, chopped green peppers, ripe olives, and spices. Cook over medium high heat, stirring occasionally, until mixture comes to a full boil. Reduce heat and simmer for five minutes. Pour sauce over chicken and serve immediately. *Yield: 4-6 servings*

Note: Garnish with chopped jalapeño peppers (optional).

Chipotle Chicken

2 cups chopped cooked chicken
2 Tablespoons slivered almonds
2 Tablespoons dark seedless raisins
2 Tablespoons sliced ripe olives
1 (15-oz.) can **HUNT'S® Tomato Sauce Special**
1 large clove garlic, minced
1½ Tablespoons brown sugar, packed
¼ cup vinegar
1 teaspoon paprika
1 teaspoon **WESSON® Oil**
½ teaspoon hickory-flavored salt
¼ teaspoon liquid smoke
⅛ teaspoon crushed red pepper
1 dozen corn tortillas
1½ cups shredded Monterey Jack cheese

In a medium bowl, combine chicken, almonds, raisins and olives; toss lightly; set aside. Blend together in a small bowl, **HUNT'S® Tomato Sauce Special**, garlic, brown sugar, vinegar, paprika, oil, hickory salt, liquid smoke and red pepper. In a 1½ quart greased casserole, arrange alternate layers of tortillas, chicken mixture, sauce mixture and cheese, *reserving ½ cup* cheese for top layer. Bake at 375°F 30 to 35 minutes. *Makes 6 to 8 servings*

Rondelet Olé

1 package (12 oz.) WEAVER® Chicken
  Rondelets—Original Recipe
1 avocado, pitted, peeled and mashed
1 Tablespoon lemon juice
¼ teaspoon salt
¼ teaspoon instant minced garlic
Dash hot pepper sauce
4 slices tomato
½ cup shredded Monterey Jack cheese

Prepare chicken patties as directed on package. Meanwhile, blend avocado, lemon juice, salt, garlic and pepper sauce. Spread on patties. Top with tomato and cheese. Bake 5 minutes longer. Garnish with lemon twist if desired.   *4 servings*

VARIATION:

Serve on warmed tostadas.

Mexican Chicken Rolls

2 whole chicken breasts, split, skinned and boned
1 4 oz. can S&W® Whole Green Chili Peppers
4 tsp. chopped S&W® Olives
½ cup shredded Monterey Jack cheese
1 egg, slightly beaten
1 cup crushed tortilla chips
¼ cup vegetable oil
1 1⅝ oz. envelope enchilada sauce mix
½ cup water
1 16 oz. can S&W® Mexican Style Stewed Tomatoes
½ cup shredded Cheddar cheese

Pound chicken breasts to flatten. On each breast, put 1 chili pepper, 1 teaspoon chopped olives and 2 tablespoons Monterey Jack cheese. Roll-up the breasts tightly and secure with toothpicks. Dip each roll into egg, then into crushed chips to coat. Heat oil in skillet and brown chicken rolls lightly. Place rolls in a shallow casserole dish. Prepare enchilada sauce according to package directions, only using ½ cup water and **Mexican Style Stewed Tomatoes**. Pour sauce over chicken rolls. Bake at 350° for 35-40 minutes. Sprinkle Cheddar cheese over top and bake an additional 5 minutes or until cheese is bubbly.   *Serves 4*

Monterey Muffin Melt

6 BAYS® English Muffins, split and lightly toasted
4 ounces alfalfa sprouts
12 slices turkey breast
12 strips bacon, cooked crisp
2 large avocados, sliced
12 slices Monterey Jack or Swiss cheese
Dipping Sauce*

Lightly butter toasted muffin halves. Layer the following on muffins: about one tablespoon of alfalfa sprouts; one slice turkey breast; one slice bacon; 2-3 slices avocado and one slice cheese. Place under broiler until cheese melts or microwave on high for 15 seconds. Garnish with fresh fruit. Eat Monterey Melt Sandwich open-faced, dipping pieces into the sauce.   *Serves 6*

*Dipping Sauce

1 cup mayonnaise
2 tablespoons Dijon mustard
1 tablespoon sherry (optional)

Using a spatula, in a small bowl, combine mustard, mayonnaise and sherry.

Mexican Fiesta Turkey Wings

1 package (2 to 3 lb.) LOUIS RICH™ Fresh Turkey
  Wings
1 cup water
1 can (15 oz.) tomato sauce with tomato bits
1 package (1¼ oz.) taco seasoning mix
1 cup (4 oz.) shredded Cheddar cheese

Remove skin that stretches between the joint of each wing; separate wing into two pieces. Rinse turkey and pat dry.

Skillet Method: Place turkey and water in skillet; bring to a boil. Cover; turn down heat. Simmer 2 hours. Pour off liquid. In small bowl combine tomato sauce and taco mix; pour over turkey. Simmer, covered, 15 minutes; sprinkle with cheese. Cover; heat 3 to 5 minutes more or until cheese melts.

Oven Method: Place turkey and water in casserole or Dutch oven; cover and bake in 350°F oven 2 hours. Remove from oven; pour off liquid. In small bowl combine tomato sauce and taco mix; pour over turkey. Bake, uncovered, 25 minutes; top with cheese and bake 5 minutes more or until cheese melts.

      Makes 2 to 4 servings

Turkey Loaf Mexicana

1 pound ground raw turkey
1 medium onion, chopped
1 green pepper, chopped
1 egg, slightly beaten
2 bread slices, crumbled
2 cups (8 ounces) shredded Cheddar cheese, divided
1 can (8 ounces) tomato sauce, divided
2 cloves garlic, minced
2 teaspoons ground cumin powder
1 teaspoon chili powder
¾ teaspoon AC'CENT® Flavor Enhancer
¼ teaspoon pepper

In large bowl combine turkey, onion, green pepper, egg, bread, 1½ cups cheese, ¼ cup tomato sauce, garlic, cumin and chili powder, AC'CENT® and pepper; mix well. Shape into a loaf and place in 1½-quart baking dish. Pour remaining tomato sauce over meat and sprinkle with remaining ½ cup cheese. Bake in a 350°F. oven 1 hour. Let stand 10 minutes before serving.

Yield: 4 servings

Mexicali Turkey Casserole

2 packages **SANWA Seasoning Flavored Noodles RAMEN PRIDE**
10¾ oz. can chicken vegetable soup
1 cup sour cream
2 to 4 tablespoons finely chopped green chiles
1½ cups chopped cooked turkey or chicken
1 cup shredded Cheddar cheese

Cook noodles in 4 cups boiling salted water 3 minutes. Drain. Combine soup, sour cream, chiles, contents of seasoning packets and turkey. Spread ½ cup of this mixture in bottom of 1½ quart casserole. Place ½ of the noodles in casserole. Spread ½ of the remaining soup mixture over noodles and sprinkle with ½ of the cheese. Repeat layers. Bake in 350° F. oven 25 minutes or until heated through.

Makes about 5 cups

Mexican-Style Duckling with Pineapple Orange Sauce

2 frozen ducklings (4 to 5 pounds each) defrosted and cut into halves or quarters
1 teaspoon salt
⅓ cup sugar
2 tablespoons cornstarch
1 can (8 ounces) pineapple tidbits or chunks
1 cup diced orange sections
⅓ cup light corn syrup
⅓ cup water
2 tablespoons grated orange rind
1 tablespoon lemon juice
6 to 8 drops **TABASCO® Sauce**, or as desired
Onion Rice (recipe follows)
Toasted slivered almonds, optional
Avocado and fresh pineapple slices for garnishing, if desired

Wash, drain and dry duckling. Sprinkle both sides with salt. Place duckling pieces, skin side up, on rack in a roasting pan. Bake in moderate oven (350°F.) until meat is tender and skin is brown and crisp, about 2 hours. Turn several times during roasting ending with skin side up. Combine and mix sugar and cornstarch in saucepan. Drain pineapple tidbits or chunks and orange sections; save juices. Add juices, corn syrup and water; stir until free of lumps. Cook until clear and thickened, stirring constantly. Stir in orange rind, lemon juice and **TABASCO® Sauce**. Add pineapple and orange; heat through. Serve duckling with Onion Rice. Sprinkle with almonds; garnish with avocado and fresh pineapple slices, if desired.

Makes 4 servings
(Continued)

Onion Rice

½ cup chopped onion
2 tablespoons cooking oil
1 cup long grain rice
Water
1 teaspoon salt
1 chicken bouillon cube

Cook onion in oil until tender, but not brown. Stir in rice. Add amount of water called for on package label, salt and bouillon cube. Bring to a boil. Cover and simmer until tender, about 15 minutes.

Yield: 4 servings

Favorite recipe from **National Duckling Council**

Seafood

Gazpacho Seafood Fillets

3 tablespoons butter
1 small onion, diced
3 medium tomatoes, diced
1 cucumber, pared and diced
1 can (8 oz.) **DOLE® Chunk Pineapple in Juice**
¼ teaspoon thyme, crumbled
¼ teaspoon garlic powder
1 tablespoon sherry
2 turbot fish fillets (3 to 4 oz. each)

Melt butter in large, heavy skillet. Sauté onion over medium-high heat until golden, about 5 minutes. Add diced tomatoes and cucumber and simmer uncovered about 10 minutes until sauce reduces and thickens. Reduce heat to low. Stir in undrained pineapple chunks and seasonings. Stir in sherry. Place fish fillets on top of sauce. Cover tightly and steam until fish is cooked, about 5 minutes (depending upon thickness of fish). Carefully remove fish from skillet with slotted spoon. Serve with sauce.

Makes 2 servings

BOOTH

Acapulco Fillets

BOOTH® 14 or 16 oz. **Fish Fillets**
¼ cup butter
1 tablespoon chili sauce
1 teaspoon lemon juice
1 tablespoon chopped parsley
1 teaspoon Worcestershire sauce
1 tomato, sliced

Place fillets in single layer on heavy duty aluminum foil large enough to fold and seal over all ingredients. Melt butter and add remaining ingredients except tomato. Spoon over fillets and top with tomato slices. Fold and seal edges tightly. Bake in a preheated 400°F oven for 30-40 minutes or until fish flakes easily with a fork. Serve on a heated platter garnished with parsley.

Baked Fish, Veracruz Style

2 pounds fresh whitefish or frozen cod fillets, thawed
    and drained
3 tablespoons vegetable oil
¼ cup onion, finely chopped
¼ cup green pepper, finely chopped
¼ teaspoon garlic, pressed or very finely chopped
2 cups **LIBBY'S®** Tomato Juice
⅛ teaspoon liquid hot pepper sauce
1 teaspoon salt
½ teaspoon sugar
⅛ teaspoon black pepper
3 tablespoons canned green chilies, drained and
    chopped
1 cup sliced stuffed green olives, drained

Preheat oven to 350°F. In a skillet, sauté onion, green pepper and garlic in oil about 3 minutes or until tender. Add tomato juice, pepper sauce, salt, sugar and pepper. Simmer uncovered for 15 minutes stirring occasionally. Cut fish into 6 serving pieces and roll (or lay flat) and place in greased 2 quart baking dish. Stir chilies and olives into sauce. Pour over fish. Bake 45 to 50 minutes or until fish flakes easily with a fork. *Yields 6 servings*

Crab Acapulco

¼ cup butter or margarine
¼ cup sifted all-purpose flour
1⅔ cups milk
¾ teaspoon salt
1 teaspoon Worcestershire sauce
Generous dash cayenne pepper
2 tablespoons **CALAVO® Fresh Lime** or **Lemon Juice**
3 tablespoons sherry wine
⅓ cup grated sharp American cheese
2 cups cooked crab meat
4 **CALAVO® Avocados**
Salt
Toasted coconut or toasted sesame seeds

Melt butter and blend in flour. Gradually blend in milk and cook and stir until smooth and thickened. Blend in salt, Worcestershire sauce, cayenne, lime juice, sherry and cheese. Add crab meat and cook just until heated. Cut avocados in halves and remove seeds and skins. Place in shallow baking dish, sprinkle with salt, and heap with crab mixture. Sprinkle with toasted coconut. Bake in slow oven (300 degrees F.) 15 minutes, just until warm. *Do not bake longer.*   *Makes 8 servings*

Rock Lobster Fra Diavolo

12 ounces frozen **SOUTH AFRICAN ROCK
    LOBSTER** Tails
⅓ cup olive oil
2 cloves garlic, chopped
1 onion, chopped
1 can (35 oz.) plum tomatoes, undrained and chopped
1 teaspoon oregano
½ teaspoon basil
½ cup red wine
Few drops **TABASCO®**

Drop frozen rock lobster into boiling salted water. When water reboils, boil for 3 minutes. (Larger 4 oz. tails, require 5 minutes boiling time). Drain immediately and drench with cold water. With scissors, remove underside membrane and pull out meat in one piece. Slice meat. In a saucepan, heat olive oil and sauté garlic and onion for 5 minutes. Stir in tomatoes, oregano, basil, wine and **TABASCO®**. Simmer for 15 minutes or until thick. Stir in rock lobster and simmer until piping hot. Spoon sauce over hot cooked spaghetti. Serve dusted with grated Parmesan cheese.
Yield: 6 servings

Favorite recipe from **South African Rock Lobster Service Corp.**

Veracruz Shrimp

1 pound fresh medium shrimp
1 large green pepper
3 tablespoons vegetable oil, divided usage
1 small onion, chopped
1 can (4 oz.) **OLD EL PASO®** Chopped Green
    Chilies
1 jar (16 oz.) **OLD EL PASO®** Taco Sauce
2 medium tomatoes, chopped
12 pimiento stuffed olives
1½ teaspoons capers
¼ teaspoon cumin
1 bay leaf
1 teaspoon salt
½ teaspoon sugar
Lime juice
Hot cooked rice

Peel shrimp and remove veins; set aside. Cut green pepper into 1½ x ½-inch strips. Heat 1 tablespoon oil in a large skillet. Add green pepper and onion. Cook until onion is translucent. Add green chilies, taco sauce, tomatoes, olives, capers, cumin, bay leaf, salt, and sugar. Bring to a boil. Reduce heat and simmer for 10 minutes. Heat 2 tablespoons of oil in a large skillet. Add shrimp. Cook over medium heat stirring constantly about 3 minutes or until shrimp turns pink. Sprinkle a few drops of lime juice over shrimp. Add sauce. Cook 2 minutes longer. Serve immediately over hot rice.
Makes 4 servings

Port Clyde Foods, Inc.

Mexican Sardine-Stuffed Tomato Cups

4 large tomatoes
Salt
Chili powder
3 (3¾-oz.) cans **PORT CLYDE** or **HOLMES**
    Sardines or **Fish Steaks in soybean oil**, drained
¼ cup chopped green chilies
½ cup seasoned poultry stuffing
1 cup shredded Monterey Jack cheese
1 cup shredded lettuce
½ cup sour cream

Preheat oven to 375°F. Cut off tops of tomatoes, making vertical saw-tooth cuts around top of tomato cups; scoop out pulp. Chop tops and pulp; drain. Drain tomato cups; sprinkle insides with salt and chili powder. Chop sardines. Blend tomato pulp, sardines, chilies, stuffing and cheese; spoon into tomato cups. Place in baking dish; add water to depth of ½ inch. Bake 25 to 30 minutes. Serve with shredded lettuce and spoonfuls of sour cream on top.

Serves 4

First-Prize Winner, Sardine Recipe Contest, Maine Seafoods Festival

Eggs & Cheese

TABASCO®

Tabasco® Huevos Rancheros

2 tablespoons salad oil
½ cup chopped onion
1 green pepper, chopped
1 tomato, peeled and chopped
1 clove garlic, minced
1 teaspoon dried leaf oregano
¾ teaspoon salt
½ to 1 teaspoon **TABASCO® Pepper Sauce**
1 can (8 ounces) tomato sauce
½ cup water
6 eggs

Heat oil in large skillet. Add onion and green pepper; cook until tender. Add tomato, garlic, oregano, salt, **TABASCO®**, tomato sauce and water. Simmer, covered, 20 minutes. Uncover. Break eggs, one at a time, into cup and slip into sauce. Cover and simmer over low heat until eggs are set, about 5 minutes. Serve over tortillas or toasted English muffins. *Yield: 6 servings*

THE ORIGINAL WORCESTERSHIRE

Huevos Rancheros

4 tablespoons oil, divided
¼ cup minced onion
1 can (1 lb.) tomatoes, broken up
2 teaspoons **LEA & PERRINS Worcestershire Sauce**
½ teaspoon salt
½ teaspoon sugar
½ teaspoon chili powder
12 tortillas
6 tablespoons butter or margarine, divided
12 eggs, divided
1 ripe avocado, peeled, pitted, and chunked

In a medium saucepan heat 1 tablespoon of the oil. Add onion; sauté for 1 minute. Add tomatoes, **LEA & PERRINS**, salt, sugar, and chili powder. Bring to boiling point. Reduce heat and simmer, uncovered, for 15 minutes. In a large skillet heat remaining 3 tablespoons oil. Add tortillas, 3 at a time; fry lightly, about 1 minute. Drain tortillas on paper towels; keep hot. In the same skillet melt 2 tablespoons of the butter. Crack 4 eggs into the skillet; fry lightly. Repeat, using remaining butter and eggs. Place an egg on each tortilla. For each serving spoon tomato sauce on an individual serving plate; place 2 egg-topped tortillas over sauce. Garnish with avocado chunks. *6 servings*

Huevos California

1 tablespoon butter or margarine
½ cup frozen **ORE-IDA® Potatoes O'Brien**
¼ teaspoon salt
¼ teaspoon chili powder
2 eggs beaten
2 tablespoons sour cream
1 tablespoon taco sauce (optional)
1 teaspoon chopped green onions
1 large (9 inch) flour tortilla

1. In skillet over medium heat (350°F.) melt butter, add potatoes, salt and chili powder; cook until potatoes are tender. Stir occasionally. Add eggs, scramble with potatoes until set.
2. Briefly warm tortilla in dry frying pan over very low heat, turning often. Place egg mixture on tortilla; top with sour cream, taco sauce and sprinkle of green onions. Fold the two sides envelope fashion, and roll up, garnish with additional sour cream and green onions. *Yield: 1 serving*

Surprise Eggs

STOKES® Green Chile Sauce with Pork
Eggs
English Muffins
Grated longhorn cheese
Optional ingredients*

Empty 2 cans **STOKES® Green Chile Sauce with Pork** into an electric skillet or a 10-12 inch skillet on top of range and heat to bubbling. Make a slight hole with a spoon and drop eggs one at a time into each hole, 4 or 5 eggs can be cooked at one time. Cover with a lid and simmer for approximately 3 or 4 minutes depending on your preference for degree of doneness. Remove with a large spoon and serve on an English muffin. Grated cheese and onion may be added.

*Optional serving suggestions: over a bed of cooked rice, toasted bread or warm flour tortilla.

Tomato Sour Cream Casserole

1 medium onion, chopped
2 tablespoons salad oil
1 1-pound 12-ounce can tomatoes
1 package Mexican style "sloppy joe" seasoning mix
1 4-ounce can green chilies, chopped
1 5½-ounce package **Nacho Cheese Flavor DORITOS® Brand Tortilla Chips**
¾ pound Monterey Jack cheese, grated
1 cup sour cream
½ cup grated Cheddar cheese

Sauté onion in oil, add tomatoes, seasoning mix and green chilies. Simmer, uncovered, 10 to 15 minutes. In a greased, deep 2-quart baking dish, layer ingredients in order: sauce, crushed **Nacho Cheese Flavor DORITOS® Brand Tortilla Chips**, Monterey Jack cheese, sauce, Monterey Jack cheese. Top with sour cream. Bake at 325°F. for 30 minutes. Sprinkle with Cheddar cheese; bake 10 minutes longer. *Makes 8 servings*

South-of-the-Border Custard Casserole

6 eggs
1 cup milk
½ cup taco sauce
1 tablespoon instant minced onion
½ teaspoon seasoned salt
1 can (4 oz.) chopped green chilies, undrained
2 cups cooked rice
1 cup (4 oz.) shredded Cheddar or Monterey Jack cheese
Parsley, optional

In large bowl beat together eggs, milk, taco sauce, onion and salt. Reserving a few pieces of chilies for garnish, stir in remaining ingredients except parsley. Pour into 8 x 8 x 2-inch baking dish. Bake in preheated 350°F. oven until knife inserted near center comes out clean, 35 to 40 minutes. Garnish with reserved chilies and parsley, if desired.   *4 to 6 servings*

Favorite recipe from the **American Egg Board**

Baked Chile Rellenos

¼ cup butter
¼ cup flour
1½ cups milk
3 eggs, separated
Ground white pepper, to taste
LAWRY'S® Seasoned Salt, to taste
9 ounces Monterey Jack cheese, sliced
2 cans (7 oz. each) whole green chiles, seeded
1 onion, thinly sliced

In a saucepan, melt butter and add flour to make a roux. Add milk slowly, beating continually, over medium heat to make a smooth thickened white sauce. Cool. Add 3 yolks; beat until well blended. Beat egg whites until stiff but not dry. Fold into white sauce. Season to taste. Pour ⅓ white sauce in bottom of 11¾ x 7½ x 2-inch baking dish. Wrap each piece of cheese within a chile and place in baking dish. Cover with sliced onion; pour remaining white sauce over. Bake in 350°F. oven 40 minutes. Serve immediately.   *Makes 6 to 8 servings*

Green Chilies Quiche

1 (9-inch) **BANQUET® Frozen Pie Crust Shell**
1 can (4 oz.) chopped green chilies, drained
¼ cup ripe olives, quartered
1 cup (4 oz.) shredded Cheddar cheese
3 eggs
½ cup milk

Spread green chilies over bottom of pie crust. Place olives on top of chilies. Sprinkle cheese on top. Beat together eggs and milk;

pour over cheese. Bake on cookie sheet in 375°F oven 30 to 35 minutes or until knife inserted 2 inches from edge comes out clean. Let stand 10 minutes before serving.

Makes 1 pie

COOKIN' GOOD™
GRADE A CHICKEN

South-of-the-Border Chicken Quiche

1 unbaked 9 inch deepdish pie shell (preferably **MRS. SMITH'S®** frozen)
1 cup shredded longhorn or Cheddar cheese
1 cup cubed **COOKIN' GOOD™ Chicken**
½ cup sliced black olives
¼ cup chopped pimientos
3 eggs
1¼ cups half and half cream
3 dashes of **TABASCO® Sauce**
⅛ teaspoon of cayenne pepper
Dash of nutmeg

Preheat oven to 375 degrees. Prick the pie shell with a fork in several places. Sprinkle the cubed chicken and black olives over the bottom of the pie shell. Using a whisk or fork, beat eggs, cream, **TABASCO®** and spices together. Pour this mixture over the chicken and olives. Sprinkle pimientos and shredded Cheddar cheese over the quiche mixture. Bake for 35-45 minutes or until a knife inserted into the center is removed clean.

Rice & Beans

Brown's Best Pintos-Mexican Delicioso

2 cups **BROWN'S BEST** Pintos—prepare using Basic Recipe*
1 lb. ground beef
4 tablespoons tomato sauce
1 tablespoon Mexican hot sauce
1 7 oz. can green chilies
1 cup stuffed green olives-sliced
¾ lb. shredded Cheddar cheese
1 tablespoon chili powder
Corn chips

Crumble beef in skillet, stir until lightly browned. Drain off fat. Add to cooked beans and mash with potato masher. Add sauce and green chilies, blend thoroughly. Turn into deep round casserole. Sprinkle olives around outer edge. Fill center with shredded cheese. Sprinkle chili powder over cheese. Bak uncovered, 350 degree oven 30 minutes or until cheese mixture is melted. Serve casserole on a warming plate with corn chips.

*Basic Recipe

1 pound **BROWN'S BEST Great Northerns, Pintos, Red Beans, Large Limas** or **Baby Limas**
12 cups water
2 teaspoons salt

Wash beans thoroughly, removing any off colored beans. Use a large heavy pot—approximately 3 times the amount of the water and beans. Bring the salted water and beans to a boiling point. Boil 2 minutes only. Cover. Remove from heat. Allow to stand 1 hour. Return to the heat and bring to a boil. Reduce the heat and simmer slowly until tender. We suggest always cooking at least 1 lb. of **BROWN'S BEST** beans at a time. If the recipe calls for less, the remainder can always be frozen to use at a later date.

Uncle Ben's®

Taco Chicken 'n Rice

6 chicken drumsticks and thighs
2 tablespoons cooking oil
1 envelope (1¼ ounces) taco seasoning mix
2 tablespoons flour
2 teaspoons salt
½ cup tomato sauce
3 cups water
1 medium onion, sliced
1 cup **UNCLE BEN'S® CONVERTED®** Brand Rice
1 tablespoon butter or margarine
3 medium zucchini, chopped
1 cup shredded Monterey Jack cheese

Brown drumsticks and thighs in oil in 12-inch skillet. Drain off excess fat. Sprinkle chicken with seasoning mix, flour, ½ teaspoon salt. Add tomato sauce and ½ cup water. Cover and cook over low heat until tender, about 45 minutes. Turn several times during cooking. Add sliced onion 15 minutes before end of cooking time. Bring remaining 2½ cups water to a boil in medium saucepan. Stir in rice, butter and 1 teaspoon salt. Cover tightly and simmer 20 minutes. Remove from heat. Stir in zucchini and remaining ½ teaspoon salt. Let stand covered until all liquid is absorbed, about 5 minutes. Serve chicken and sauce over rice. Sprinkle with cheese.

Makes 6 servings

Sour Cream Frijoles

1 can (15½ oz.) **VAN CAMP'S® Mexican Style Chili Beans**
½ cup sour cream
½ cup American cheese, grated
¼ cup green onions, chopped (including tops)

Heat Chili Beans in saucepan. Stir in sour cream and heat just to boiling. Pour into serving bowl and garnish with cheese and onion.

Makes 4 servings

Ranchero Beans

2 cans (1 pound each) **HEINZ Vegetarian Beans in Tomato Sauce**
⅓ cup **HEINZ Tomato Ketchup**
3 tablespoons chopped onion
1 tablespoon light brown sugar
1 tablespoon molasses or dark corn syrup
¼ teaspoon salt
⅛ to ¼ teaspoon hot pepper sauce
2 slices bacon, partially cooked

Combine all ingredients except bacon in a 1 quart casserole. Top with bacon. Bake, uncovered, in 375°F. oven, 1 hour, stirring occasionally. *Makes 4-6 servings (about 3½ cups)*

Spanish Rice with Deviled Smithfield Ham and Mushrooms

1 cup of rice, uncooked
¾ cup chopped onions
½ cup chopped green peppers
½ cup chopped celery
8 oz. fresh mushrooms (sliced thinly and sautéed in butter)
4 Tbsp. of butter or salad oil
½ tsp. salt
Dash of black pepper
Dash of cayenne
1 #2½ can tomatoes (3½ cups)
3 oz. **AMBER BRAND Deviled SMITHFIELD Ham**

Cook rice until tender and drain. Sauté the chopped onions, green peppers, and celery in butter or oil until tender. Add mushrooms and seasoning, then the **Deviled SMITHFIELD Ham**. Cook this mixture until blended for about 3 minutes. Add tomatoes, and simmer for 20 minutes and then pour in rice. Turn into well-greased casserole and bake in moderate oven for about 30 minutes.

A clove of garlic or a teaspoon of chili powder adds to the flavor of this dish. *Serves 6 or 7*

Lipton®

Lipton® Rice Olé

2 slices bacon
⅓ cup chopped onion
¼ cup finely chopped green pepper
1½ cups water
2 envelopes **LIPTON® Tomato Cup-a-Soup**
1 cup uncooked instant rice
½ teaspoon garlic salt

In medium skillet, cook bacon until crisp; drain, reserving 2 tablespoons drippings. Crumble and reserve bacon. Add onion and green pepper to skillet; cook until tender. Add water and bring to a boil. Stir in instant tomato soup mix, rice, garlic salt and reserved bacon; cover and remove from heat. Let stand 5 minutes.
Note: Recipe can be doubled. *Makes 3 to 4 servings*

GRANDMA'S MOLASSES

Quickie Bean Bake

½ cup **GRANDMA'S® Unsulphured Molasses**
3 tablespoons vinegar
3 tablespoons prepared mustard
½ teaspoon **TABASCO® Pepper Sauce**
3 cans (1 pound each) baked beans in tomato sauce
1 can (1 pound) kidney beans, drained
½ pound frankfurters, cut in 1-inch pieces
1 cup diced cooked ham
1 medium onion, chopped, divided

Mix molasses, vinegar, mustard and **TABASCO®**. Add to baked beans, kidney beans, frankfurters and ham in 3-quart casserole. Add half of chopped onion; mix well. Bake in 375°F. oven 1 hour. Stir before serving. Sprinkle remaining chopped onion around edge of casserole. *Yield: 8 servings*

Butter Buds®

Pinto Bean Casserole

¾ cup (about 5 ounces) dried pinto beans
1 quart cold water
½ teaspoon salt
1 clove garlic, pierced with a toothpick
1 bay leaf
4 ounces uncooked spinach noodles
1 tablespoon vegetable oil
½ cup diced celery
¼ cup chopped onion
½ teaspoon basil
½ teaspoon dry mustard
½ teaspoon thyme
¼ teaspoon sage
1 packet **BUTTER BUDS®**
¼ cup chopped pimiento
Freshly ground pepper to taste
¼ cup (1 ounce) grated mozzarella cheese

Pick over beans to remove any blemished ones. Wash in cold water. Drain. Soak in water overnight. Transfer beans and liquid to saucepan. Add salt, garlic, and bay leaf. Bring to a boil. Reduce heat and simmer, covered, until beans are tender, about 1 hour. Drain, reserving liquid from cooked beans. Cook noodles as directed on package. When tender, remove from heat, drain, and rinse noodles with cold water.

Preheat oven to 350° F. Heat oil in large skillet. Add celery, onion, basil, mustard, thyme, and sage. Sauté until vegetables are tender, about 5 minutes. Measure 2 cups liquid from cooked beans. Add with **BUTTER BUDS®**, pimiento, and pepper to celery-onion mixture in skillet. Mix thoroughly. Remove garlic and bay leaf. Add beans and noodles. Mix well. Transfer mixture to non-stick baking dish. Sprinkle top with cheese. Cover with foil. Bake about 30 minutes, or until cheese melts. *4 servings*

PER SERVING (1 cup): Calories: 305 Protein: 12gm
Carbohydrate: 46 gm Fat: 5 gm Sodium: 250mg

Chili Cheese Rice

1 cup enriched uncooked long-grain rice
16 ounces plain yogurt
6 ounces chopped green chilies
Salt
Pepper
2 ounces **COUNTY LINE® Cheddar Cheese**, cubed
4 ounces **COUNTY LINE® Monterey Jack Cheese**, sliced and cut into strips

Cook rice in medium-size saucepan following label directions. Stir in yogurt and chilies, small amounts of salt and pepper, and **COUNTY LINE® Cheddar Cheese** and **COUNTY LINE® Monterey Jack Cheese**. Cover and allow the cheeses to melt. *Serves 6*

Koops Spanish Rice

¼ lb. bacon
1 small onion
3 cups cooked rice
2 8 oz. cans tomato sauce
1 tsp. **KOOPS' Extra Strong Mustard**

Cut bacon in small pieces; brown lightly; remove grease; add finely chopped onion; brown lightly. Add remaining ingredients and simmer for five minutes. Serve hot.

Uncle Ben's®

Gazpacho Style Rice

2½ cups water
1 cup **UNCLE BEN'S® CONVERTED® Brand Rice**
1 tablespoon butter or margarine
1½ teaspoons salt
1 chicken bouillon cube, crushed
2 green onions, sliced
1 garlic clove, minced
2 tablespoons olive oil
1 tablespoon red wine vinegar
Dash of pepper
1 medium tomato, chopped
1 medium green pepper, chopped
1 small cucumber, peeled and chopped
1 to 1½ cups garlic or onion croutons

Bring water to a boil in medium saucepan. Stir in rice, butter, 1 teaspoon salt and bouillon cube. Cover tightly and simmer 20 minutes. Remove from heat. Let stand covered until all liquid is absorbed, about 5 minutes. Meanwhile, combine green onions, garlic, oil, vinegar, pepper and remaining ½ teaspoon salt; mix well. Cover and let stand while rice is cooking. Stir into hot cooked rice. Serve bowls of tomato, green pepper, cucumber and croutons separately. Sprinkle vegetables and croutons over rice as desired. *Makes 6 servings*

Rice Olé

1 cup *each* chopped onions and green peppers
½ cup chopped celery
3 tablespoons butter, margarine or oil
2 teaspoons chili powder
2¼ teaspoons garlic salt
1 can (14½ to 16 ounces) tomatoes (drain, chop and reserve juice)
3 cups cooked **BLUE RIBBON Rice**

Cook onions, green peppers and celery in butter until vegetables are soft but not brown. Add seasonings, tomatoes, including all juice and **BLUE RIBBON Rice.** Simmer, stirring occasionally, until flavors are blended and liquid is absorbed. *Makes 6 servings*

MICROWAVE METHOD:
Combine onions, green peppers, celery and butter in a 2-quart microproof casserole. Cover and cook on HIGH (maximum power) for 9 minutes. Add seasonings, tomatoes, ⅔ cup reserved juice and **BLUE RIBBON Rice.** Cover and cook on HIGH 9 minutes, stirring at 3 minute intervals. Allow to stand 5 minutes.*

*Standing time is important in microwave cooking. Food continues to cook after it is removed from the oven.

Smoky Chili Rice

2 slices bacon
¼ cup chopped onion
¼ cup chopped green pepper
1 can (15 oz.) canned chili without beans
1 bag **SUCCESS® Rice**
½ roll (9 oz. roll) pasteurized processed cheese with bacon, sliced
¾ cup crushed corn chips

Cook rice according to package directions. Cook bacon until crisp. Remove and crumble. Sauté onion and green pepper in bacon drippings. Drain off excess fat. Stir in chili and heat.

In lightly buttered 1 quart casserole, layer the rice, slices of cheese, and chili. Repeat layers. Sprinkle the combination of corn chips and crumbled bacon on top. Bake at 400° F. for 15 minutes.
Serves 4 to 6

Monterey Rice Olé

2 cups uncooked rice
1 can (28 ounce) **REDPACK Whole Tomatoes in Juice**
2 tablespoons butter
1 onion, chopped
2 tablespoons flour
1 cup milk
¼ teaspoon salt
⅛ teaspoon pepper
1 can (4 ounce) green chilies, diced
½ pound Monterey Jack cheese, sliced
Paprika

Cook rice according to package directions. Drain tomatoes, saving juice. Cut up tomatoes. Melt butter in skillet; sauté onion until translucent. Stir in flour and cook until bubbly; remove from heat. Stir in milk, saved tomato juice, salt and pepper. Return to heat,

stirring constantly until thickened. Remove from heat; add tomatoes and chilies and combine with cooked rice. Turn half of rice mixture into baking dish, about 12 x 8 x 2-inch, top with half of cheese. Spoon remaining rice into casserole and top with remaining cheese. Garnish with paprika. Bake immediately, or cover and refrigerate until about an hour before serving. Bake uncovered in 350 degree F. oven about 20 to 25 minutes or until heated completely through. *Serves 8*

Note: May be made ahead and frozen.

Kidney Beans with Rice

½ pound **GOYA® Kidney Beans**
5 cups of water
1 green pepper
3 ounces bacon
1 **GOYA® Chorizo** cut into ½-inch slices
4 tablespoons **GOYA® Olive Oil**
2 medium onions
1 tablespoon **GOYA® Garlic Powder**
4 teaspoons **GOYA® Salt**
¼ teaspoon **GOYA® Ground Oregano**
1 **GOYA® Bay Leaf**
1 pound **CANILLA Rice**

Soak beans overnight. Cook in the same water until tender. Drain and reserve 3 cups of the liquid. Chop the bacon and fry in oil until the fat starts melting. Add the Chorizo, ground onions and chopped pepper, sauté for a few seconds. Mix with the beans, water, bay leaf, garlic powder, oregano and salt. When boiling begins, add the rice and cook, covered, over medium heat until it is tender. *Serves 8*

Mexican Bean and Rice Pie

3 cups cooked **BLUE RIBBON Rice**
2 eggs slightly beaten
2 cups grated cheese (Monterey Jack)
8 ounces ground sausage (pork or beef)
1 cup chopped onions
3½ cups cooked pinto beans
1 teaspoon garlic salt
1 tablespoon finely chopped jalapeño or ½ cup diced green chili
¼ cup each barbecue sauce, chopped tomatoes, green pepper strips, and/or jalapeño slices

Combine **BLUE RIBBON Rice**, eggs and 1 cup cheese. Press firmly into a greased 8½ inch x 11 inch cake pan. Bake at 450 degrees for 25 minutes or until lightly brown. While crust is baking, cook sausage and onions in medium-sized skillet until sausage is done and onions are soft but not brown. Stir to crumble meat. Set aside. Drain beans thoroughly. Remove ½ cup whole beans and reserve; mash remainder. Add garlic salt, jalapeños and barbecue sauce to mashed beans. Spread evenly over baked rice crust. Cover with sausage mixture. Sprinkle top with remaining cheese, reserved whole beans and garnish as desired with chopped tomatoes, green peppers and/or jalapeño slices. Bake 15 minutes longer.
Makes 6 to 8 servings

Vegetables

Frijoles and Zucchini Bake

2 tablespoons oil
1 cup diced zucchini
½ cup chopped green pepper
½ cup chopped onion
¼ pound ground beef
¼ cup dry white wine
2 tablespoons tomato paste
¼ cup dark raisins
½ teaspoon salt
¼ teaspoon each pepper, cinnamon and allspice
1 can (16-ounces) pork and beans in tomato sauce
1 package (8-ounces) pre-sliced Cheddar cheese slices
Corn or tortilla chips

Heat oil in a large skillet. Add zucchini, green pepper and onion. Sauté until tender, about 5 minutes. Push vegetables to one side, add meat and brown. Stir in wine, tomato paste, raisins, salt, pepper, cinnamon and allspice. Cook 3 minutes, stirring occasionally. Stir in beans and continue cooking until heated through. Line four 6-ounce casseroles with half of the cheese. Spoon meat mixture into casseroles. Top with remaining cheese. Place in a 400°F. oven for 5 minutes or until cheese melts and is bubbly. Serve with corn chips or tortilla chips.   *Makes 4 servings*

Favorite recipe from **Michigan Bean Commission**

Campbell's

Cactus Corn

4 slices bacon
¼ cup green pepper strips
1 can (11 ounces) **CAMPBELL'S Condensed Cheddar Cheese Soup**
3 cups cooked whole kernel corn
½ cup drained chopped canned tomatoes

In saucepan, cook bacon until crisp; remove and crumble. Pour off all but 2 tablespoons drippings. Cook green pepper in drippings until tender. Add soup, corn and tomatoes. Heat; stir occasionally. Garnish with bacon.   *Makes about 4 cups, 4 servings*

TripleSec

Valencia Mushrooms

½ lb. fresh mushrooms, very thinly sliced
4 ribs celery very thinly sliced
2 Tbsp. lemon juice
3 Tbsp. **HIRAM WALKER Triple Sec**
Finely chopped parsley

Combine ingredients and chill for several hours. Serve on bibb lettuce. Garnish with lemon slices.   *Serves 4*

ORTEGA

Tomato Chile Fill-Ups

6 large, firm tomatoes
1 large avocado
1 can (4 oz.) **ORTEGA Diced Green Chiles**
3 tablespoons mayonnaise
1 teaspoon lemon juice
1 tablespoon finely chopped celery
1 tablespoon minced onion
Lettuce

Wash tomatoes and scoop out pulp (reserve pulp). Set tomatoes upside down to drain while you mash and mix avocado with 4 tablespoons of chiles (reserve remaining chiles), 2 tablespoons of the mayonnaise, lemon juice, celery and onion. Fill tomatoes with mayonnaise-vegetable mixture. Set stuffed tomatoes on salad plates lined with lettuce leaves. Mix tomato pulp and reserved chiles with additional mayonnaise for dressing. Serve dressing separately in a bowl.   *Serves 6*

VARIATION:

Add canned baby shrimp to stuffing or use as a garnish ring around base of tomatoes for a change of pace. Create additional variations by using your favorite garnish.

Mexican Stuffed Zucchini

3 medium zucchini
1 can (10 oz.) **OLD EL PASO® Enchilada Sauce**
½ cup water
1 slice bacon, chopped
¼ cup chopped green pepper
1 can (4 oz.) **OLD EL PASO® Chopped Green Chilies**
1 small onion, chopped
1 cup chopped mushrooms
1 clove garlic, minced
½ cup canned corn
¼ cup sliced black olives
1½ cups cooked rice
1 cup **OLD EL PASO® Taco Sauce**
1 egg, beaten
¼ teaspoon salt
⅛ teaspoon pepper
½ cup grated dry Parmesan cheese

Preheat oven to 325°F. Slice the zucchini in half lengthwise and scoop out and discard seeds and pulp. Combine enchilada sauce and water in a large shallow baking dish. Then place the zucchini in the dish skin-side down and steam in oven under foil for 30 minutes or until tender. Meanwhile, sauté bacon; drain. Add green pepper, green chilies, onion, mushrooms, and garlic. Cook until onion is translucent. Remove from heat and add corn, olives, rice, taco sauce, egg, salt and pepper. Mix together. Scoop mixture into zucchini shells and top with cheese. Cover again with foil and bake until zucchini is tender, approximately 35 minutes.   *Makes 6 servings*

Chili con Queso Potatoes

1 package **BETTY CROCKER®** Au Gratin Potatoes
1 cup shredded process American cheese (about 4 ounces)
½ cup chili sauce
1 to 2 tablespoons diced hot jalapeño peppers
1 teaspoon Worcestershire sauce
3 or 4 drops red pepper sauce

Prepare potatoes as directed on package for Stove-Top Method. Stir in remaining ingredients; cook and stir 5 minutes longer.

6 servings

MICROWAVE METHOD:
Mix potatoes, Sauce Mix and 3 cups boiling water in 3-quart round microwavable casserole. Cover with waxed paper and microwave on high (100%) 10 minutes; stir. Cover and microwave until potatoes are tender, 7 to 10 minutes. Stir in remaining ingredients. Cover and microwave until hot, 2 to 4 minutes longer.

HIGH ALTITUDE DIRECTIONS (3500 to 6500 feet): Prepare potatoes as directed in high altitude directions on package for Stove-Top Method. Continue as directed in recipe.

Tater Tots® Mexicana

3-4 cups frozen **ORE-IDA® TATER TOTS®***
1 can (16 ounce) stewed tomatoes
¼ tsp. oregano, crumbled
1 cup commercial sour cream
2 tablespoons milk
1 tablespoon chopped canned green chiles
½ tsp. salt
½ cup grated Cheddar cheese

1. Preheat oven to 375° F.

2. Turn frozen **TATER TOTS®** into 1½-quart shallow baking dish. Mix with tomatoes and oregano.

3. In small bowl, stir sour cream, milk, chiles and salt together. Spoon over top. Sprinkle with cheese.

4. Bake 25 minutes. *Yield: 4-6 servings*

*May also be prepared with the following **ORE-IDA®** products:

> **TATER TOTS® with Bacon**
> **TATER TOTS® with Onion**

MICROWAVE METHOD:
Follow above recipe using these preparation directions:

1. Place microwave on high setting and set out a shallow microwave casserole dish.

2. In casserole dish combine tomatoes and oregano; mix in **TATER TOTS®**. In bowl mix together sour cream, milk, chiles and salt; spoon over top of **TATER TOTS®** mixture.

3. Microwave casserole 14-15 minutes or until center is hot and bubbly. Rotate dish twice during cooking. Sprinkle with cheese and let stand 5 minutes before serving.

Gazpacho Tomato Relish

2¾ cups peeled, chopped tomatoes
1 green pepper, coarsely chopped
1 medium onion, coarsely chopped
1 tablespoon prepared horseradish
1 teaspoon salt
⅔ cup **HENRI'S** Bacon 'n Tomato French Dressing

1. Combine tomatoes, green pepper, onion, horseradish and salt. Let stand 1 hour.
2. Drain off excess liquid.
3. Stir in **HENRI'S** Bacon 'n Tomato French Dressing.
4. Chill. *Makes 2½ cups relish*

Desserts

Rum Flan

1¼ cups sugar, divided usage
4 eggs
2 cups **PET®** Evaporated Milk
2 cups milk
2 tablespoons dark rum or 1 tablespoon rum flavoring
¼ teaspoon salt

Preheat oven to 350°F. In skillet place ½ cup sugar over low heat, watching carefully, allow sugar to melt and turn brown (caramelize). Pour caramelized sugar into flan pan, or 2-quart casserole, or souffle dish. Rotate until bottom is covered. Beat eggs and remaining ¾ cup sugar in large mixing bowl. Add evaporated milk, milk, rum and salt. Mix well. Pour milk mixture into mold. Place the mold in a large pan. Pour warm water into the larger pan halfway up the sides of the mold. Bake about 1 hour and 45 minutes to 2 hours, or until knife inserted halfway into flan comes out clean (do not pierce bottom). Chill for several hours. Unmold. *Makes 6-8 servings*

EAGLE® BRAND

Classic Almond Flan

¼ cup firmly packed light brown sugar
¾ cup (3 ounces) blanched slivered almonds, toasted
1 (14-ounce) can **EAGLE®** Brand Sweetened Condensed Milk (NOT evaporated)
1 cup (½ pint) whipping cream
5 eggs
½ teaspoon almond extract
Additional toasted almonds, optional

Preheat oven to 325°. In 8-inch round layer cake pan, sprinkle sugar; set aside. In blender container, grind nuts; add sweetened condensed milk, ½ cup cream, eggs and extract. Blend thoroughly. Pour into pan. Set in larger pan of hot water, 1-inch deep. Bake 40 to 45 minutes or until knife inserted near center comes out clean. Chill thoroughly (about 3 hours); turn out of pan. Beat remaining cream for garnish; top with additional toasted almonds if desired. Refrigerate leftovers. *Makes 8 to 10 servings*

Mexican Flan

8 eggs, beaten
⅔ cup granulated sugar
¼ teaspoon salt
2 cans (13 oz. each) **MILNOT**®
2 teaspoons vanilla
½ cup brown sugar (or 1 cup white sugar caramelized)*

Beat sugar and salt with eggs. Add **MILNOT**® and vanilla; blend well. Press brown sugar into bottom of loaf pan (approx. 9x5x3-inch); carefully pour custard over sugar. Place pan in shallow pan of hot water (about 1 inch from top of custard). Bake in 350° oven for 1 hour or until knife inserted near center comes out clean. Chill well before unmolding on a flat dish or platter. (The brown sugar makes the sauce).   *Makes about 10 servings*

Note: This can be made in 8-10 custard cups. Reduce baking time to 30-35 minutes.

*To caramelize white sugar, heat sugar in heavy skillet until liquid and golden brown. Glaze bottom and sides of pan or custard cups; fill with custard and bake.

Jacquin's Mocha Mousse

1 6-ounce package semi-sweet chocolate bits
2 eggs
2 tablespoons very strong hot coffee
2 tablespoons **JACQUIN'S Creme de Cafe** or **JACQUIN'S Coffee Brandy**
½ teaspoon **JACQUIN'S Creme de Cacao**
¾ cup scalded milk

Put all ingredients into blender jar and blend at high speed for 2 minutes. Pour into individual dessert cups and chill for at least 2 hours.   *Serves 4*

Chocolate Mousse

1 envelope unflavored gelatin
2 tablespoons unsweetened cocoa
2 eggs, separated
2 cups low-fat milk, divided
5 packets **SWEET 'N LOW**®
1½ teaspoons vanilla

In medium-size saucepan, mix gelatin and cocoa. In separate bowl, beat egg yolks with 1 cup milk. Blend into gelatin mixture. Let stand 1 minute to soften gelatin. Stir over low heat until gelatin is completely dissolved, about 5 minutes. Add remaining milk, **SWEET 'N LOW**®, and vanilla. Pour into large bowl and chill, stirring occasionally, until mixture mounds slightly when dropped from spoon. In separate large bowl, beat egg whites until soft peaks form; gradually add gelatin mixture and beat until doubled in volume, about 5 minutes. Chill until mixture is slightly thickened. Turn into dessert dishes or 1-quart bowl and chill until set.   *8 servings*

Per Serving (½ cup): Calories: 65; Fat: 3g

Low Sodium Chocolate Mousse

1 pkg. (12 oz.) semi-sweet chocolate pieces
½ cup boiling water
2 teaspoons **ANGOSTURA**® **Aromatic Bitters**
4 egg yolks
4 egg whites, stiffly beaten

In a blender, combine chocolate pieces, boiling water, **ANGOSTURA**® and egg yolks. Whirl until smooth and cool to room temperature. Beat egg whites in a bowl until stiff. Fold in chocolate mixture. Spoon mixture into serving dishes. Chill for several hours. Serve with demi-tasse.   *Serves 6*

Per serving: Sodium 37 mg; Calories 325

Mocha Spanish Cream

1 envelope unflavored gelatin
¼ cup cold water
2 eggs, separated
1½ cups low-fat milk, scalded
1 teaspoon instant decaffeinated coffee
½ teaspoon vanilla
6 packets **SWEET 'N LOW**®, divided

In small bowl, soften gelatin in cold water. In top of double boiler, beat egg yolks; blend in milk. Cook, stirring constantly, over hot water until mixture thickens slightly. Add softened gelatin and coffee; stir until dissolved. Remove from heat. Stir in vanilla and 3 packets **SWEET 'N LOW**®. Chill until mixture is consistency of unbeaten egg whites.

In large bowl, beat egg whites with electric mixer until foamy. Add remaining **SWEET 'N LOW**®. Beat until stiff. Fold chilled custard mixture into egg whites. Pour into serving dishes. Chill until set.   *4 servings*

| PER SERVING (½ cup): | Calories: 105 | Protein: 9gm |
| Carbohydrate: 7gm | Fat: 5gm | Sodium: 90mg |

Chocolate Meringue Torte

8 egg whites
1¼ cups sugar
2 cups finely-chopped toasted pecans
3 pints **BREYERS**® Chocolate Ice Cream, softened*
½ cup heavy cream
¼ cup cocoa
2 tablespoons sugar

Grease and flour four baking sheets. Trace an 8-inch circle on each. Beat egg whites until foamy. Gradually add sugar and continue beating to stiff peaks. Fold in pecans. Divide mixture evenly among pans; spread evenly on each circle. Bake at 325°F. 30 minutes or until golden. Cool on pan for 10 minutes. Remove to racks and cool completely.

Place one meringue on serving platter. Spread with 1 pint ice cream. Repeat with two more layers. Place remaining meringue on top. Freeze 6 hours or overnight. Remove from freezer 10 minutes before serving. Combine cream, cocoa and sugar. Whip to soft peaks. Force through pastry tube on top of torte.

Makes one 8-inch torte

*Soften ice cream until easily scooped

Margarita Soufflé

1 can (20 oz.) DOLE® Sliced Pineapple in Juice
½ cup water
1 package (3 oz.) lime flavored gelatin
¼ teaspoon salt
4 eggs, separated
2 tablespoons lime juice
½ teaspoon grated lime peel
¼ cup tequila
¼ cup triple sec
1½ cups heavy cream, whipped

Drain pineapple reserving juice. Heat juice and water to boil. Stir in gelatin and salt until dissolved. Beat egg yolks well. Slowly add to warm mixture, stirring constantly. Cook over low heat, stirring, 3 to 4 minutes. Remove from heat and let cool. Stir in lime juice, peel, tequila and triple sec. Chill until mixture mounds on spoon. Beat egg whites until stiff peaks form. Fold into gelatin mixture. Fold in whipped cream. Place 7 pineapple slices on edge around sides of 1½-quart clear glass soufflé dish. Make a wax paper collar to extend 2 inches above rim of dish; brush with oil. Gently pour gelatin mixture into prepared dish. Chill until firm, 4 hours or overnight. Garnish with remaining 3 slices of pineapple and lime slices, if desired. Remove collar to serve.

Makes 6 to 8 servings

Bananas with Mexican Chocolate Sauce

(A Dessert Fondue)

½ cup light cream
½ teaspoon instant coffee (dry granules)
2 bars (4 ounces each) sweet cooking chocolate
½ cup coffee liqueur
Chilled CHIQUITA® Bananas
Pound cake squares

Heat cream in dessert size fondue pot over medium to low heat. Dissolve coffee in cream. Break chocolate into squares and heat and stir in cream until melted and blended. Stir in coffee liqueur. Continue to keep hot over low heat.

Cut peeled bananas into 1-inch slices. Spear on fondue fork and dip into sauce. Spear cake squares on fork and dip into sauce.

Makes 2 cups

Note: Sauce adheres better to cold bananas than those at room temperature. Place fruit in refrigerator at least an hour before peeling and serving. Allow one banana per person.

KNOX®
Rice with Milk Pudding

(Arroz con Leche)

1 envelope KNOX® Unflavored Gelatine
½ cup sugar
3 eggs
2 cups milk
1 teaspoon vanilla extract
2 cups cooked rice
1 cup (½ pt.) whipping or heavy cream, whipped
½ cup diced mixed candied fruit

In large saucepan, mix unflavored gelatine with sugar; blend in eggs beaten with milk. Let stand 1 minute. Stir over low heat until gelatine is completely dissolved, about 5 minutes. Stir in vanilla and rice. Pour into large bowl and chill, stirring occasionally, until mixture mounds slightly when dropped from spoon.

Fold in whipped cream and fruit. Turn into 6-cup mold or bowl; chill until firm. Garnish with maraschino cherries. Serve, if desired, with caramel or fruit sauce.

Makes about 12 servings

Cocoa Pudding

¼ cup HERSHEY'S® Cocoa
⅔ cup sugar
3 tablespoons cornstarch
¼ teaspoon salt
2¼ cups milk
2 tablespoons butter
1 teaspoon vanilla

Combine cocoa, sugar, cornstarch and salt in medium saucepan; gradually blend milk into dry ingredients. Cook over medium heat, stirring constantly, until mixture boils; boil and stir one minute. Remove from heat; blend in butter and vanilla. Pour into individual serving dishes. Chill. Garnish as desired.

4 to 5 servings

Mexican Pudding

Spoon into dessert dishes:
    4 cans (5 oz. each) DEL MONTE PUDDING CUP
    Lemon Cream Pudding

Place in freezer to chill.

Toast:
    ¼ cup chopped nuts

Garnish each serving with ground cinnamon and toasted chopped nuts.

✳️KAMORA®
Kamocha Cake

1 18½ oz. chocolate cake mix
1 3⅝ oz. chocolate pudding mix
4 eggs
½ cup vegetable oil
½ cup cold water
½ cup + extra dash of **KAMORA**®

Combine above ingredients. Pour into a greased 13 inch x 9 inch oblong pan. Bake in a 325° oven approximately 45 minutes. Test with toothpick. Let cool. Then frost with:

1 can chocolate frosting
2 Tbsp. **KAMORA**®
2 Tbsp. powdered sugar

Combine above. Mix thoroughly. Frost cake.

Brandy Cake de los Reyes

Brandied Fruits and Syrup (recipe follows)
2 cups chopped pecans
1 cup flaked coconut
½ cup **THE CHRISTIAN BROTHERS**® Brandy
3½ cups sifted flour
1½ teaspoons baking powder
½ teaspoon salt
8 eggs
2 cups butter or margarine, softened
1½ cups granulated sugar
½ cup packed brown sugar
1 teaspoon vanilla
¼ cup toasted blanched almonds
Powdered sugar

Prepare Brandied Fruits and Syrup at least 24 hours and up to 1 week in advance; set aside. In 1-quart bowl combine pecans, coconut and brandy. Toss and set aside. Combine flour, baking powder and salt; set aside. With electric mixer at high speed beat eggs until light and lemon-colored, about 5 minutes; set aside. In large bowl cream butter, sugars and vanilla with mixer at medium speed, until light and fluffy, about 5 minutes. Add eggs. Beat 2 minutes. Gradually add flour mixture, beating at low speed just to blend. Stir in pecan mixture to blend thoroughly. Turn into greased and floured 10 x 4-inch tube pan. Smooth top. Bake in 350 degree oven about 1 hour 20 minutes until pick inserted into center comes out clean. If needed, cover with aluminum foil to prevent over-browning. Cool in pan on rack 20 minutes. Remove from pan and place on serving plate top side up. Drain Brandied Fruits; reserve syrup. While still warm brush exposed surfaces of cake several times with syrup, reserving about 3 tablespoons. Arrange fruits and almonds on top of cake. Drizzle with remaining syrup. Just before serving, dust with powdered sugar. To serve place some of the fruits on each plate and accompany with a slice of cake. *Makes 24 servings*

Brandied Fruits and Syrup

In glass or plastic container with tight-fitting lid combine 1 cup dried pear halves, ⅔ cup dried apricot halves and ½ cup candied red cherries; set aside. In 1-quart saucepan combine 1 cup sugar, ¾ cup **THE CHRISTIAN BROTHERS**® Brandy and ¼ cup water. Stir and bring to boiling over medium heat. Simmer 5 minutes. Pour over fruits; stir. Cover and let stand at room temperature.

Maryland Club.Coffee
Taste of Texas Mocha Cake

1 cup sifted cake flour
¼ cup cocoa
½ teaspoon baking soda
½ teaspoon ground cinnamon
¼ teaspoon baking powder
¼ teaspoon salt
¼ cup shortening
¾ cup sugar
1 egg, unbeaten
⅓ cup buttermilk
⅓ cup brewed **MARYLAND CLUB**® Coffee
½ teaspoon vanilla
Mocha Cream Frosting (recipe follows)

Sift flour with cocoa, soda, cinnamon, baking powder, and salt. Cream shortening; add sugar gradually, creaming together until light and fluffy. Add egg, beating thoroughly. Combine buttermilk, coffee, and vanilla. Add flour mixture to egg mixture, alternately with liquid, beating after each addition until smooth.

Pour batter into well-greased and floured 9-inch square pan or Texas-shaped pan. Bake in moderate oven (350°F.) 35 minutes or until cake springs back when pressed lightly. Cool; frost with Mocha Cream Frosting.

Mocha Cream Frosting

1¼ to 1½ cups sifted confectioners' sugar
2 tablespoons cocoa
⅛ teaspoon salt
¼ cup butter or margarine
2-3 tablespoons brewed **MARYLAND CLUB**® Coffee
¼ teaspoon vanilla

Sift sugar, cocoa, and salt together. Cream butter and gradually add part of sugar mixture, blending after each addition, until light and fluffy. Add remaining sugar alternately with coffee, until of right consistency to spread, beating after each addition until smooth. Blend in vanilla. Makes about 1½ cups frosting, or enough to frost top and sides of one 9-inch square or Texas-shaped cake.

Chocolate Chiffon Cake

2 squares unsweetened chocolate
¼ cup water
4 egg yolks
¾ cup sugar
1 cup **SALERNO**® Graham Cracker Crumbs
1 teaspoon baking soda
½ teaspoon baking powder
½ teaspoon salt
¼ cup water
¼ cup oil
1 teaspoon vanilla
4 egg whites
¼ teaspoon cream of tartar
¼ cup sugar

Melt chocolate with water over low heat; cool to lukewarm. I small bowl of mixer, beat egg yolks with ¾ cup sugar until thic and lemon colored, about 2 minutes. Add graham cracker crumbs, baking soda, baking powder, salt, water, oil, vanilla and chocolate mixture. Beat at low speed until blended, then at medium speed for 5 minutes. With clean beaters, beat egg whites and cream of tartar in large bowl of mixer until foamy. Gradually add sugar while beating at high speed. Beat until stiff peaks form. Fold ¼ of egg whites into chocolate mixture to lighten. Fold chocolate mixture into remaining egg whites. Pour into ungreased 10 inch tube pan. Bake in preheated 325° oven 45 to 50 minutes. Invert; cool. Run a spatula around edge and center tube; remove from pan. Serve with ice cream.

KITCHENS OF Sara Lee
Chocolate Flan

1 frozen **SARA LEE Chocolate Cake** (single layer)
½ cup water
1 teaspoon lemon juice
2 sliced bananas
⅓ cup orange marmalade, melted

Cut frozen Cake lengthwise into 2 layers. Place top cake half on serving plate, frosting up, stack on remaining layer. Dip bananas in mixture of water and lemon juice; drain. Arrange bananas in overlapping design on cake top. Drizzle marmalade over bananas. Thaw at room temperature about 30 minutes.

Makes 6-8 servings

Banana Rum Cake
(Torta Al Ron)

2¼ to 2¾ cups unsifted all purpose flour
1 cup sugar
1 package active dry yeast
1 teaspoon salt
¼ cup milk
½ cup butter or margarine
3 eggs (at room temperature)
1 cup mashed **CHIQUITA® Banana** (2 to 3 bananas)
¼ cup water
¼ cup orange juice
¼ cup rum
⅔ cup (approximately) apricot jam
Glacé cherries, blanched whole almonds, if desired for garnish

Combine ½ cup flour with ½ cup sugar, yeast and salt in a large bowl. Heat milk with butter until warm. Butter does not need to be completely melted. Add gradually to flour mixture. Beat at medium speed of mixer for 2 minutes. Scrape sides of bowl several times. Add another ½ cup flour, eggs and mashed bananas and beat another 2 minutes at high speed of mixer. Scrape sides of bowl several times. Gradually stir in enough of the remaining flour to make a thick batter. (It should hold its shape when lifted with spoon.)

Cover and let set in a warm place about 1 hour or until bubbly. Stir down batter. Turn into a well greased and floured 2-quart Turk's head, ring mold, or **Bundt**® cake pan. Cover and let rise in warm place about 1½ hours or until doubled in bulk. Bake in 350°F oven 30 to 35 minutes. Unmold on rack and let cool.

Meanwhile boil remaining ½ cup sugar and water together for 1 minute. Cool. Add orange juice and rum.

Place cooled cake on a serving plate. Carefully pour rum sauce over cake. Let set until all sauce is absorbed. Spread apricot jam over cake. If desired, the cake may be garnished with glacé cherries and blanched almonds.

Makes 1 ring mold or 12 servings

Note: If any cake is left over, it should be stored loosely covered, at room temperature. It will keep this way for several days. Leftover cake may also be frozen. Freeze, then wrap in moisture-proof freezer paper. Label, date and return to freezer. Storage time, about 30 days.

Coffee Liqueur Pie

1 **PET-RITZ® Regular Pie Crust Shell**, baked
1 small can (5.33 fl. oz.) **PET® Evaporated Milk**
½ cup semi-sweet chocolate pieces
2 cups miniature marshmallows
⅓ cup chopped almonds, toasted*
⅓ cup coffee liqueur
1 container (12 oz.) **PET® WHIP Non-Dairy Whipped Topping**, thawed
Maraschino cherries

Combine evaporated milk and chocolate pieces in heavy 1-quart saucepan. Cook over low heat, stirring occasionally, until chocolate melts completely and mixture thickens. Stir in marshmallows until melted. Remove from heat. Add almonds. Pour into a 2-quart bowl and refrigerate until cool (about 20 to 30 minutes), stirring twice. Add coffee liqueur. Fold in whipped topping. Spoon into baked pie shell. Freeze several hours until firm. Remove from freezer 10 minutes before serving for ease in cutting. If desired, garnish with additional **PET® WHIP**, chopped almonds and maraschino cherries.

Makes 8 servings

*To toast almonds: Place almonds on baking sheet in preheated 350°F oven, stirring frequently until almonds are lightly toasted, about 10 minutes.

Margarita Pie

½ cup margarine or butter
1¼ cups finely crushed **WISE® Mini Pretzels**
¼ cup sugar
1 (14-ounce) can **EAGLE® Brand Sweetened Condensed Milk** (NOT evaporated milk)
⅓ cup **REALIME® Lime Juice from Concentrate**
2 to 3 tablespoons tequila
2 tablespoons triple sec or other orange-flavored liqueur
1 cup (½ pint) **BORDEN® Whipping Cream**, whipped
Additional whipped cream and pretzels for garnish, optional

In small saucepan, melt margarine; stir in pretzel crumbs and sugar. Mix well. Press crumbs on bottom and up side of buttered 9-inch pie plate; chill. In large bowl, combine **EAGLE® Brand**, **REALIME®**, tequila and triple sec; blend well. Fold in whipped cream. Turn into prepared crust. Freeze or chill until firm (4 hours in freezer; 2 hours in refrigerator). Before serving, garnish with whipped cream and pretzels if desired. Refrigerate or freeze leftovers.

Makes one 9-inch pie

California Dreaming Avocado Pie

1 KEEBLER® READY-CRUST® Graham Cracker
  Pie Crust
1 3-oz. package lemon gelatin
1 8-oz. container vanilla yogurt
1 11-oz. can mandarin oranges, drained
2 tablespoons sliced almonds
2 ripe avocados, peeled and mashed

Prepare gelatin according to package instructions. Refrigerate until slightly thickened (egg white consistency); add yogurt and refrigerate until firm, about 30 minutes. Add avocados to mixture. Beat with electric mixer until mixture is fluffy, fold in oranges, reserving 10 for garnish, and refrigerate until mixture is spoonable. Mound into pie crust and garnish with sliced almonds and remaining oranges. *Serves 8*

Pineapple Empanadas

1 cup **SMUCKER'S Pineapple Preserves**
⅓ cup finely chopped sliced almonds
¼ teaspoon almond extract
2 cups unsifted all-purpose flour
1½ teaspoons baking powder
½ teaspoon salt
½ cup vegetable shortening
About 6 tablespoons ice water

In small bowl, combine Pineapple Preserves, almonds and extract for the filling. In large bowl, combine flour, baking powder and salt. Cut in shortening with pastry blender until mixture resembles coarse crumbs. Sprinkle with water; mix with fork until dough clings together. Add a little more water if dough is dry. Gather dough into a ball and knead just until smooth, about 10 times. Roll dough on lightly floured surface to ⅛-inch thickness. Cut into 4-inch circles with floured cookie cutter. Place about 1 tablespoon pineapple filling in center of each circle leaving an edge all around. Moisten edge with water. Fold in half and press edges to seal. Press edge with tip of a floured fork. Reroll trimmings; continue to cut and fill. Place turnovers on lightly greased baking sheet. With fork, prick top of each turnover. Bake in preheated 400° F. oven about 15 minutes or until golden.

VARIATION:

For variety, try apricot or peach preserves, instead of pineapple.

Kahlúa® Wafers/Kahlúa® Dip

Kahlúa® Wafers

2¼ cups sifted all-purpose flour
¾ cup sugar
½ tsp. salt
¼ tsp. baking powder
¾ cup soft butter
3 Tbsp. KAHLÚA®
½ tsp. instant coffee crystals
1 tsp. vanilla

Resift flour with sugar, salt and baking powder. Blend in butter. Mix **KAHLÚA®**, instant coffee and vanilla, and let stand a minute to soften coffee crystals. Add to flour mixture and blend to a moderately stiff dough. Chill ½ hour or longer. Roll on lightly floured board to about ⅛-inch thickness. Cut with floured cutter. Bake above oven center in moderately hot oven (375 degrees F) 5 to 7 minutes until edges are very lightly browned. Cool and store in airtight container. *Makes about 5 dozen 2¼-inch cookies*

Kahlúa® Dip

1 8-ounce package cream cheese
¼ cup KAHLÚA®
2 Tbsp. light cream
2 Tbsp. chopped toasted blanched almonds

Soften cream cheese. Gradually beat in **KAHLÚA®** and cream until mixture is smooth. Stir in almonds. Serve with **KAHLÚA®** Wafers and fruit, such as strawberries, bananas, pineapple chunks or fresh apple wedges for dipping. *Makes 1⅓ cups*

Snow Balls

1 cup (2 sticks) butter
½ cup sifted confectioners' sugar
2 cups sifted cake flour
1 tablespoon milk
1 teaspoon vanilla
3 CLARK® Bars (1¼ ounces each), chopped
Sifted confectioners' sugar

Beat butter and confectioners' sugar until creamy and fluffy. Add flour, milk and vanilla; mix well. Stir in candy. Chill thoroughly. Shape into 1-inch balls. Place 2 inches apart on ungreased cookie sheet. Bake at 375° for 12 to 15 minutes. While still warm, sprinkle with confectioners' sugar. *3 dozen*

AMARETTO di SARONNO®

Frosted Oranges Saronno

2 cups water
¾ cup sugar
Grated rind and juice of 1 lemon
½ cup AMARETTO DI SARONNO®
2 egg whites, stiffly beaten
6 large oranges
½ cup flaked coconut
⅓ cup AMARETTO DI SARONNO®
1 egg white, beaten until foamy
Granulated sugar

In a saucepan, combine water and sugar. Bring mixture to a boil and boil for 5 minutes. Remove from heat and stir in lemon rind and juice and **AMARETTO DI SARONNO®**. Pour mixture into a freezer container and freeze until mushy. Pour mixture into a bowl and beat until smooth. Fold in beaten egg whites. Replace in container, cover and freeze until hard. With a sharp knife, slice off the top of each orange. With knife, cut out pulp of orange leaving shell whole. Remove membrane from pulp, cut into sections, and place in a bowl. Fold in coconut and **AMARETTO DI**

SARONNO®. Chill. Brush outside of orange shell and top of orange with slightly beaten egg white. Dip into granulated sugar until well coated. Let dry at room temperature until crusty. When ready to serve, fill orange shell with orange mixture. Spoon **AMARETTO DI SARONNO®** ice on top of filled shell. Replace top of orange and serve garnished with fresh mint sprigs, if desired. Serve at once. *Makes 6 servings*

Brandy Piñata Pralines

2 cups granulated sugar
1 cup packed brown sugar
½ cup **THE CHRISTIAN BROTHERS®** Brandy
½ cup whipping cream
¼ cup butter or margarine
2 cups salted peanuts

In 3-quart saucepan stir sugars, brandy, cream and butter over medium heat to dissolve sugars. Bring to boiling and cook without stirring until mixture reaches 234 degrees on candy thermometer. Remove from heat. Add peanuts and beat 2 to 3 minutes just until mixture begins to look opaque. Spoon immediately onto baking sheets lined with waxed paper, to form 3-inch patties. Cool; peel off paper and store in airtight container.

Makes 18 pralines (about 1½ pounds)

Quick Pralines

¼ cup water
2 tablespoons butter or margarine
1 cup firmly-packed **COLONIAL®** Light Golden Brown Sugar
1 cup **COLONIAL®** Confectioners' Sugar
½ teaspoon vanilla extract
¾ cup chopped pecans

In medium saucepan, bring water and butter to a boil; stir in sugars. Return to boiling; boil and stir 1 minute. Remove from heat; stir in vanilla and pecans. Beat until mixture begins to thicken slightly. Immediately drop from teaspoon onto wax paper. Cool. Store in covered container.

Makes about 1½ dozen pralines

Sopapaillas

1 envelope (¼ ounce) dry yeast
⅓ cup warm water
¾ cup milk
3 tablespoons vegetable shortening
3 cups all-purpose flour, stirred before measuring
½ teaspoon baking powder
½ teaspoon salt
1 cup **SMUCKER'S** Apple Jelly
3 tablespoons water
½ teaspoon ground cinnamon
Oil for deep frying

In a large bowl, sprinkle yeast over warm water. Stir until yeast dissolves. In a small saucepan, heat milk until just warm. Stir warm milk and shortening into yeast. Add 2½ cups of the flour, baking powder and salt; stir until well mixed. Add more flour until a stiff dough forms. Gather dough and knead about 2 minutes on lightly floured surface until dough is smooth, adding more flour if necessary. Cover dough on surface with inverted bowl; let stand 10 minutes. Meanwhile, in small saucepan, combine Apple Jelly, 3 tablespoons water and cinnamon; heat to boiling, stirring until jelly is smooth. Keep warm over low heat. Into a 3-quart or larger saucepan, pour oil to fill pan a third full. Heat over medium heat to 425° F. Roll dough with floured rolling pin to a 10 x 12-inch rectangle, about ¼ inch thick. From the 10-inch edge, cut lengthwise into four 2½ inch strips. Then, cut strips crosswise to form six 2-inch pieces. Drop the pieces, about 5 at a time, top side down, into the hot oil. (Dough puffs better when top side is dropped first.) Fry until golden brown, about 3 minutes, turning frequently with slotted spoon. Drain on paper towels. Return oil to 400-425° F. before frying more. Continue to fry all pieces. Drizzle sopapaillas with apple jelly mixture and serve warm.

Makes 24 fritters or 8 servings

VARIATION:

Break sopapaillas in half, fill insides with your favorite flavors of **SMUCKER'S** jam or preserves. Omit apple jelly sauce.

Dessert Fruit Taco

2 cups melon balls or cubes (cantaloupe, watermelon, honeydew)
2 cups strawberries, washed, hulled and halved
2 cups pineapple chunks
1 cup seedless green grapes, halved
1 orange, peeled, sectioned and sliced into ½-inch pieces
1 banana, peeled and sliced
1 kiwi, peeled and sliced
½ cup fresh raspberries
1 box (10 shells) **LAWRY'S®** Super Taco Shells*
¼ cup powdered sugar
¼ teaspoon cinnamon
Shredded coconut, to garnish

Combine all fruit in large bowl; chill. Sift together powdered sugar and cinnamon. Heat Taco Shells according to package directions. Lightly sift sugar mixture over inside and outside of heated Taco Shells. Fill each shell with 1 cup mixed fruit; garnish with coconut.

Makes 10 Super Tacos

*May use **LAWRY'S®** Taco Shells, regular size. Fill regular shells with ⅓ cup mixed fruit.

Beverages

The Rose's®
Marguerita

Mix 1½ oz. White Tequila, 1 oz. **ROSE'S®** Lime Juice, ½ oz. Triple Sec. Shake with crushed ice and strain into Marguerita glass edged with salt. For an easy way to edge the glass, pour ½ oz. **ROSE'S®** Lime Juice into a saucer, dip glass edge into the **Lime Juice**, then dip into another saucer of Marguerita salt.

STOCK

Margarita

Moisten the rim of a cocktail glass with lemon or lime peel. Gently coat the entire rim with salt. Stir with ice one jigger of **OLÉ Tequila**, ½ oz. **STOCK Triple Sec**, and the juice of ½ lemon or lime. Strain and serve.

Galliano Margarita

½ oz. **LIQUORE GALLIANO®**
1½ oz. Tequila
2 oz. Sweet and Sour Mix, or Margarita Mix
(1 oz. fresh lime or lemon juice may also be used)

Blend or shake with ice and pour into champagne glass. Salt rim if desired.

Souverain

Light Sangria

5 cups **SOUVERAIN® Chardonnay**
2 cups chilled club soda
¼ cup **DRY SACK® Sherry**
½ cup sugar
1 orange, thinly sliced
1 lemon, thinly sliced
1 apple, cut in wedges
6 maraschino cherries with stems

In a large pitcher combine **SOUVERAIN® Chardonnay**, club soda, **DRY SACK® Sherry** and sugar; stir until sugar dissolves. Mix in orange, lemon, apple and cherries. Serve chilled with ice cubes if desired. *Makes 2 quarts*

REALIME

White Sangria

1 cup sugar
1 (8-ounce) bottle **REALIME® Lime Juice from Concentrate**, chilled
1 (750mL) bottle sauterne, chilled
2 tablespoons orange-flavored liqueur
1 (32-ounce) bottle club soda, chilled
Orange slices, optional

In pitcher, dissolve sugar in **REALIME®**; stir in sauterne and orange-flavored liqueur. Just before serving, add club soda and orange slices. Serve over ice. *Makes about 2 quarts*

Blonde Sangria

Place ⅓ to ½ cup sugar in punch bowl or large pitcher. Cut 2 or 3 thin slices from the centers of each of 2 lemons and 2 oranges; set slices aside. Squeeze juice and pulp from end pieces of fruit into bowl and mix well to dissolve sugar. Add 1 half-gallon **ALMADÉN Mountain Rhine Wine** or **Chablis**. Add ice and 1 pint club soda. (Do not stir after adding soda.) Garnish with slices of fruit. *Serves 6 to 8 (about 20 4-ounce servings)*

Lipton.

Sangria Cup

¼ cup **LIPTON® 100% Instant Tea** Powder
½ cup sugar
1 bottle (⅘ qt.) rosé wine
1 cup sliced strawberries
1 orange, sliced
½ lemon, sliced
2 bottles (7 oz. ea.) club soda, chilled

In large pitcher, mix 100% instant tea powder with sugar. Stir in wine and fruit. Just before serving, add soda. Serve with ice. *Makes about 5 servings*

Five Alive™ Sangria

1 orange, thinly sliced
1 lemon, thinly sliced
1 lime, thinly sliced
½ cup granulated sugar
1 bottle (5th) **TAYLOR® California Cellars Chablis**
1 carton (32 oz.) **SNOW CROP® FIVE ALIVE™ Fruit Beverage**
½ cup apricot brandy

Place the sliced fruit in large pitcher. Add the sugar and mash with spoon to release juice from fruit. Add the wine, **FIVE ALIVE™** and brandy. Mix well and chill. Serve over ice, if desired, and garnish with additional fruit slices.
Makes 16 servings (about ½ cup each)

Tequila Sunrise

1½ ounces tequila
4 ounces orange juice
¾ ounce **GIROUX® Grenadine**
Ice cubes

Pour tequila and orange juice over ice. Stir. Add **GIROUX® Grenadine**. Let it sink to the bottom. Watch the sunrise.
8-ounce glass

South of the Berry

Shake together:

1 cup GIBSON Currant Wine
1 oz. orange curaçao
¼ cup orange juice
1 oz. Tequila Gold (or Dark Rum)

Pour over ice; garnish with squeeze of lime. (If you prefer, with Tequila, salt the rim!)   *Serves 2*

Brandied Mexican Chocolate

1 cup instant chocolate-flavored beverage powder
1 teaspoon ground cinnamon
¾ cup water
3 cups half and half
2 cups THE CHRISTIAN BROTHERS® Brandy
¾ cup amaretto
Cinnamon sticks

In large bowl whisk together chocolate beverage powder, ground cinnamon and water until smooth. Stir in half and half, brandy and amaretto. Cover and chill. Stir before serving. Ladle over ice into stemmed glasses. Or, heat just to boiling; pour into small cups. Serve with cinnamon stick stirrers.

Makes 12 servings (about 4½ ounces each)

Brazilian Iced Chocolate

2 squares (1 oz. each) unsweetened chocolate
¼ cup sugar
1 cup double strength hot coffee
2½ cups milk
1½ cups COCA-COLA®
Whipped cream or ice cream

Melt chocolate in top of double boiler over hot water. Stir in sugar. Gradually stir in hot coffee, mixing thoroughly. Add milk and continue cooking until all particles of chocolate are dissolved and mixture is smooth, about 10 minutes. Pour into jar, cover and chill. When ready to serve, stir in chilled **COCA-COLA®**. Serve over ice cubes in tall glasses. For a beverage, top with whipped cream. For a dessert, add a scoop of vanilla ice cream.

Makes 5 cups

Sealtest®
Mocha Float

2½ cups milk, scalded
2½ cups hot coffee
SEALTEST® Heavenly Hash Ice Cream

Combine milk and coffee; chill. Gradually add to 1 cup ice cream stirring until smooth. Place scoop of ice cream in each glass; fill with coffee mixture. Garnish with whipped cream, if desired.

6 to 8 servings

Coffee Frangelico®

¾ oz. **KAHLÚA®**
2 tsp. **FRANGELICO® Liqueur**
¾ oz. vodka
3 oz. crushed ice

Combine **KAHLÚA®, FRANGELICO®** and vodka. Stir well. Pour over ice and serve in old fashioned glass.

Durkee®
Mexicano Olé

1½ cups strong hot coffee
4 teaspoons sugar
¼ teaspoon **DURKEE Ground Cinnamon**
2 tablespoons **DURKEE Chocolate Extract**

Combine all ingredients and pour into small cups. Top with spicy whipped topping.*   *Makes 3 to 4 servings*

*Spicy Whipped Topping

1 cup frozen whipped topping, thawed
¼ teaspoon **DURKEE Ground Cinnamon**
⅛ teaspoon **DURKEE Ground Nutmeg**

Combine all ingredients.

Laced Brazilian Mocha

¼ cup instant coffee
1 square (1-oz.) unsweetened chocolate cut up
¾ cup hot water
¼ cup sugar
Dash of salt
1 cup milk
1 cup light cream
¼ cup **BÉNÉDICTINE Liqueur**
Sweetened whipped cream

Combine instant coffee and chocolate in a deep saucepan. Add hot water; stir until chocolate is melted. Stir in sugar and salt. Bring mixture to a boil. Gently boil mixture about 5 minutes, stirring frequently.

Scald milk and cream. Stir into chocolate mixture. Remove from heat. Stir in **BÉNÉDICTINE**. Beat with rotary beater until frothy. Serve immediately topped with sweetened whipped cream.   *Serves 4*

Comfort Mocha

1 teaspoon instant cocoa or hot chocolate
1 teaspoon instant coffee
1 jigger (1½ oz.) **SOUTHERN COMFORT®**

Put ingredients in mug. Fill with hot water. Stir. Top with small marshmallows.

Acknowledgments

The Editors of CONSUMER GUIDE® wish to thank the companies and organizations listed for use of their recipes and artwork. For further information contact the following:

A.1., *see* Heublein Inc.

Ac'cent International, Inc.
Pet Incorporated
400 S. Fourth St.
St. Louis, MO 63166

Alaska King Crab Marketing Board, *see* Pacific Kitchens

Almadén Vineyards
P.O. Box 5010
San Jose, CA 95150

Amaretto Di Saronno®—Foreign Vintages, Inc.
95 Madison Avenue
New York, NY 10016

Amber Brand Deviled Smithfield Ham, *see* Smithfield Ham and Products Co.

American Beauty®—The Pillsbury Company
608 2nd Avenue South
Minneapolis, MN 55402

American Egg Board
1460 Renaissance Dr.
Park Ridge, IL 60068

American Soybean Association
P.O. Box 27300
St. Louis, MO 63141

Angostura International Ltd.
Rahway, NJ 07065

Arga's Mexican Food Products
2825 Pellissier Pl.
City of Industry, CA 91744

Argo®/*Kingsford's*®, *see* Best Foods

Armour and Company
111 W. Clarendon
Phoenix, AZ 85077

Aunt Nellie's Foods Inc.
Clyman, WI 53016

Azteca Corn Products Corp.
4850 S. Austin
Chicago, IL 60638-1491

Baltimore Spice Company, The
P.O. Box 5858
Baltimore, MD 21208

Banquet Foods Corp.
Ballwin, MO 63011

Bays Home Service Institute
500 N. Michigan Ave.
Chicago, IL 60611

Bénédictine, *see* Julius Wile Sons & Co., Inc.

Best Foods
Englewood Cliffs, NJ 07632

Betty Crocker®, *see* General Mills, Inc.

Birds Eye®, *see* General Foods

Bisquick®, *see* General Mills, Inc.

Blue Ribbon Rice—American Rice, Inc.
P.O. Box 2587
Houston, TX 77252

Bob Evans Farm
P.O. Box 07863, Station G
Columbus, OH 43207

Booth Fisheries Corp.
2 North Riverside Plaza
Chicago, IL 60606

Borden Inc.
180 E. Broad St.
Columbus, OH 43215

Breyers®, *see* Kraft Inc.

Bridgford Foods Corp.
1308 N. Patt St.
Anaheim, CA 92801

Brilliant Seafood, Inc.
315 Northern Ave.
Boston, MA 02210

Broadcast®—John Morrell & Co.
191 Waukegan Rd.
Northfield, IL 60093

Brown's Best—Kelley Bean Co.
Morrill, NE 69358

Budweiser®—Anheuser-Busch, Inc.
St. Louis, MO 63118

Bumble Bee®, *see* Castle & Cooke Foods

Butter Buds®, *see* Cumberland Packing Corp.

Butterball® *Swift's Premium*®, *see* Swift & Co.

Calavo Growers of California
Box 3486, Terminal Annex
Los Angeles, CA 90051

California Brandy Advisory Board
426 Pacific Avenue
San Francisco, CA 94133

California Iceberg Lettuce Commission
P.O. Box 3354
Monterey, CA 93940

Campbell Soup Co.
Camden, NJ 08101

Canilla, *see* Goya Foods Corp.

Castle & Cooke Foods
P.O. Box 3928
San Francisco, CA 94119

Chef Boy-Ar-Dee®—American Home Foods
685 Third Ave.
New York, NY 10017

Chicken of the Sea®, *see* Ralston Purina Co.

Chilli Man®, *see* Milnot Company

Chiquita Brands, Inc.
15 Mercedes Dr.
Montvale, NJ 07645

Christian Brothers®, *The*—Fromm and Sichel, Inc.
P.O. Box 7448
San Francisco, CA 94120

Clark, D. L., Company
503 Martindale St.
Pittsburgh, PA 15212

Coca-Cola Company, The
P.O. Drawer 1734
Atlanta, GA 30303

Coca-Cola Company, The—Foods Division
P.O. Box 2079
Houston, TX 77001

Colonial Sugars, Inc.
P.O. Box 1646
Mobile, AL 36633

Consolidated Dairy Products Co.
Box C 19099
Seattle, WA 98109

Cookin' Good™—Showell Farms
Showell, MD 21862

Corn Chex®, *see* Ralston Purina Co.

County Line Cheese Company
Auburn, IN 46706

Cream of Wheat, *see* Nabisco Brands, Inc.

Creamette Co., The
428 North First St.
Minneapolis, MN 55401

Cumberland Packing Corp.
2 Cumberland Street
Brooklyn, NY 11205

Dannon Company, Inc., The
22-11 38th Ave.
Long Island City, NY 11101

Dari-Lite, *see* Consolidated Dairy Products Co.

Darigold, *see* Consolidated Dairy Products Co.

Del Monte Corporation
P.O. Box 3575
San Francisco, CA 94105

Dole®, *see* Castle & Cooke Foods

Dore Rice Mill, The
Crowley, LA 70526

Doritos®, *see* Frito-Lay, Inc.

Dry Sack®, *see* Julius Wile Sons & Co., Inc.

Durkee Foods
16651 Sprague Road
Strongsville, OH 44136

Eagle® *Brand*, *see* Borden Inc.

El Rio®—Reese Finer Foods Inc.
Box 38
Dayton, OH 45449

Elam Mills
2625 Gardner Road
Broadview, IL 60153

Ellis®, *see* Stokes Canning/Ellis Foods

Featherweight®—Chicago Dietetic Supply, Inc.
405 E. Shawmut Ave.
La Grange, IL 60525

Figaro Co., The
P.O. Box 10875
Dallas, TX 75207

Filippo Berio—Berio Importing Corp.
P.O. Box 239
Scarsdale, NY 10583

Florida Avocado Administrative Committee, *see* Pacific Kitchens

Florida Department of Natural Resources
3900 Commonwealth Blvd.
Tallahassee, FL 32303

Frangelico®—William Grant & Sons, Inc.
130 Fieldcrest Ave.
Edison, NJ 08817

French, R. T., Co.
Rochester, NY 14609

Frito-Lay, Inc.
P.O. Box 35034
Dallas, TX 75235

Furman Canning Co.
Northumberland, PA 17857

Gebhardt Mexican Foods
P.O. Box 7130, Station A
San Antonio, TX 78285

General Foods
White Plains, NY 10625

General Mills, Inc.
Minneapolis, MN 55440

Gerber Products Company
Fremont, MI 49412

Gibson Wine Company
P.O. Drawer E
Elk Grove, CA 95624

Gioia Macaroni Co., Inc.
P.O. Box 237
Buffalo, NY 14240

Giroux®—Iroquois Grocery Products, Inc.
Stamford, CT 06905

Gold Medal®, *see* General Mills, Inc.

Goya Foods Corp.
100 Sea View Dr.
Secaucus, NJ 07094

Grandma's®—Duffy-Mott Co., Inc.
370 Lexington Ave.
New York, NY 10017

Hamburger Helper®, *see* General Mills, Inc.

Health Valley Natural Foods
700 Union Street
Montebello, CA 90640

Heinz U.S.A.
P.O. Box 57
Pittsburgh, PA 15230

Hellmann's®, *see* Best Foods

Henri's Food Products Co. Inc.
2730 W. Silver Spring Dr.
Milwaukee, WI 53209

Hershey Foods Corp.
Hershey, PA 17033

Heublein Inc.—Grocery Products Group
Farmington, CT 06032

Hillshire Farm®, *see* Kahn's and Company

Hiram Walker & Sons, Inc.
P.O. Box 33006
Detroit, MI 48232

Holland House Brands Co.
Ridgefield, NJ 07657

Holmes, *see* Port Clyde Foods, Inc.

Hunt-Wesson Kitchens
1645 W. Valencia Dr.
Fullerton, CA 92634

International Multifoods
Box 2942
Minneapolis, MN 55402

Iowa Beef Industry Council
123 Airport Road
Ames, IA 50010

Jacquin, Charles, et Cie., Inc.
2633 Trenton Ave.
Philadelphia, PA 19125

James River Smithfield, *see* Smithfield Ham and Products Co.

Jeno's
525 Lake Avenue South
Duluth, MN 55802

Jimmy Dean Meat Company, Inc.
1341 W. Mockingbird Ln.
Dallas, TX 75247

Jones Dairy Farm
Ft. Atkinson, WI 53538

Julius Wile Sons & Co., Inc.
Lake Success, NY 11042

Kahlúa®—Maidstone Wine & Spirits, Inc.
70 Universal City Plaza
Universal City, CA 91608

Kahn's and Company
3241 Spring Grove Ave.
Cincinnati, OH 45225

Kamora®—James B. Beam Distilling Co.
500 N. Michigan Ave.
Chicago, IL 60611

Kaukauna®, *see* International Multifoods

Keebler Company
One Hollow Tree Lane
Elmhurst, IL 60126

Kellogg Company
Battle Creek, MI 49016

Kingsford's®, *see* Best Foods

Kitchen Bouquet®—Clorox Company
P.O. Box 24305
Oakland, CA 94623

Knox® *see* Lipton, Thomas J., Inc.

Koops—Holland Mills, Inc.
625 N. Sacramento Blvd.
Chicago, IL 60612

Kraft Inc.—Dairy Group
P.O. Box 7830
Philadelphia, PA 19101

Kretschmer, *see* International Multifoods

La Preferida, Inc.
3400 W. 35th St.
Chicago, IL 60632

La Sauce®, *see* Armour and Company

Land O'Lakes, Inc.
Arden Hills, MN 55440

Lawry's Foods, Inc.
570 West Avenue 26
Los Angeles, CA 90065

Lea & Perrins, Inc.
Fair Lawn, NJ 07410

Libby, McNeill & Libby, Inc.
200 S. Michigan Ave.
Chicago, IL 60604

Lindsay International Inc.
5327 W. Hillsdale Drive
Visalia, CA 93277

Lipton, Thomas J., Inc.
Englewood Cliffs, NJ 07632

Liquore Galliano®—"21" Brands, Inc.
75 Rockefeller Plaza
New York, NY 10019

Louis Rich Company
Div. of Oscar Mayer Foods Corp.
Madison, WI 53707

Martha White Foods Inc.
P.O. Box 58
Nashville, TN 37202

Marukan Vinegar (U.S.A.) Inc.
7755 E. Monroe St.
Paramount, CA 90723

Maryland Club®, see Coca-Cola Company,
Foods Division

Mazola®, see Best Foods

Merkt Cheese Co., Inc.
Bristol, WI 53104

Michigan Bean Commission
P.O. Box 22037
Lansing, MI 48909

Milnot Company
Litchfield, IL 62056

Minute®, see General Foods

Morton Salt
110 N. Wacker Dr.
Chicago, IL 60606

Mu Tofu Shop
1735 W. Greenleaf
Chicago, IL 60626

Nabisco Brands, Inc.
625 Madison Avenue
New York, NY 10022

Nalley's Fine Foods
3303 S. 35th
Tacoma, WA 98411

National Duckling Council
503 S. Oak Park Avenue
Oak Park, IL 60304

National Hot Dog & Sausage Council
400 W. Madison
Chicago, IL 60606

National Pork Producers Council
P.O. Box 10383
Des Moines, IA 50306

Nestlé Company, The
White Plains, NY 10605

Ocean Spray Cranberries, Inc.
Plymouth, MA 02360

Old El Paso®, see Pet Incorporated

Ole´, see Schenley Affiliated Brands Corp.

Open Pit®, see General Foods

Ore-Ida Foods, Inc.
P.O. Box 10
Boise, ID 83707

Ortega, see Heublein Inc.

Oscar Mayer Foods Corporation
Madison, WI 53707

Pacific Kitchens
300 Elliott Avenue West
Seattle, WA 98119

Pepperidge Farm, Inc.
Norwalk, CT 06856

Perdue Farms Inc.
Salisbury, MD 21801

Pet Incorporated
400 S. Fourth St.
St. Louis, MO 63166

Port Clyde Foods, Inc.
Falmouth, ME 04105

Potato Buds®, see General Mills, Inc.

Premium, see Nabisco Brands, Inc.

ProTen®—Swift Independent Packing Co.
115 W. Jackson
Chicago, IL 60604

Ragu´®—Chesebrough-Pond's Inc.
Trumbull, CT 06611

Ralston Purina Co.
St. Louis, MO 63188

ReaLemon®, see Borden Inc.

ReaLime®, see Borden Inc.

Red Star®—Universal Foods Corporation
433 E. Michigan
Milwaukee, WI 53201

Redpack—California Canners and Growers
3100 Ferry Building
San Francisco, CA 94106

Regina, see Heublein Inc.

Roman Meal Co.
2101 S. Tacoma Way
Tacoma, WA 98409

Rosarita Mexican Foods Co.
P.O. Box 1427
Mesa, AZ 85201

Rose's®—L. Rose & Co.
1200 High Ridge Road
Stamford, CT 06905

S&W Fine Foods, Inc.
P.O. Box 5580
San Mateo, CA 94402

Salerno-Megowen Biscuit Co.
7777 N. Caldwell
Chicago, IL 60648

San Giorgio-Skinner, Inc.
One Chocolate Avenue
Hershey, PA 17033

Sanwa Foods Inc.
530 Baldwin Park
City of Industry, CA 91746

Sara Lee, Kitchens of
500 Waukegan Rd.
Deerfield, IL 60015

Sargento Cheese Company Inc.
Plymouth, WI 53073

Schenley Affiliated Brands Corp.
888 Seventh Avenue
New York, NY 10106

Sealtest®, see Kraft Inc.

Shake N' Bake®, see General Foods

Sizzlean®, see Swift & Company

Skinner®, see San Giorgio-Skinner, Inc.

Skippy®, see Best Foods

Smithfield Ham and Products Co., The
Smithfield, VA 23430

Smucker, J. M., Company, The
Orrville, OH 44667

Snow Crop®, see Coca-Cola Company,
Foods Division

South African Rock Lobster Service Corp.
450 Seventh Ave.
New York, NY 10123

Southern Comfort
1220 N. Price Rd.
St. Louis, MO 63132

Souverain®, see Julius Wile Sons & Co., Inc.

Stock, see Schenley Affiliated Brands Corp.

Stokely-Van Camp, Inc.
941 N. Meridian St.
Indianapolis, IN 46206

Stokes Canning/Ellis Foods
1575 Alcott St.
Denver, CO 80204

Success®—Riviana Foods Inc.
P.O. Box 2636
Houston, TX 77001

Sunkist Growers, Inc.
P.O. Box 7888
Van Nuys, CA 91409

Sunshine Biscuits, Inc.
245 Park Avenue
New York, NY 10017

Sweet 'N Low®, see Cumberland
Packing Corp.

Sweetlite™—Batterlite Whitlock Inc.
P.O. Box 259
Springfield, IL 62705-0259

Swift & Company
Oak Brook, IL 60521

Tabasco®—McIlhenny Co.
Avery Island, LA 70513

Taco-Mate®—Fisher Cheese Co.
Wapakoneta, OH 45895

Tennessee Pride®—Odom Sausage Co., Inc.
Madison, TN 37115

3-Minute Brand®—National Oats
Company Inc.
1515 H. Avenue NE
Cedar Rapids, IA 52402

Top Ramen®—Nissin Foods (USA) Co., Inc.
2001 W. Rosecrans Avenue
Gardena, CA 90249

Two Fingers®, see Hiram Walker & Sons, Inc.

Tyson Foods, Inc.
Springdale, AR 72764

Uncle Ben's Foods
P.O. Box 1752
Houston, TX 77001

Van Camp's®, see Stokely-Van Camp, Inc.

Weaver, Victor F., Inc.
403 S. Custer Ave.
New Holland, PA 17557

Wesson®, see Hunt-Wesson Kitchens

Whoppers®—Leaf Confectionary, Inc.
1155 N. Cicero
Chicago, IL 60651

Wise®, see Borden Inc.

Wolf Brand Products
2929 Carlisle St.
Dallas, TX 75204

Wyler's®, see Borden Inc.

Yoplait®, see General Mills, Inc.

Index